Embroidering COTTAGE GARDEN FLOWERS

JENNI KIRKHAM

Kangaroo Press

Acknowledgments

My thanks go to my photographer Gordon Kirkham and to Gail and Brian Costigan for the loan of their home for several of the settings.

I am also grateful for the help and encouragement received from the manufacturers and importers of embroidery threads and materials, including DDCC, DMC, Coats Patons and Ireland Needlecraft. Special thanks also to Australian thread producers Louise Howland of Rajmahal, Jennifer Newman of Minnamurra Threads and Julie Hanks of Gumnut Yarns for providing yarns.

First published in 1996 by Kangaroo Press Pty Ltd
3 Whitehall Road Kenthurst NSW 2156 Australia
PO Box 6125 Dural Delivery Centre NSW 2158
Printed in Hong Kong through Colorcraft Ltd

ISBN 0 86417 568 8

Contents

Introduction 4

1 Wisteria shadow box 5

2 Calico mouse sachet 7

3 Sweet pea pillowcase 10

4 Rose and initial crystal jar lid 13

5 Topiary rose tree 15

6 Cross-stitch sampler 19

7 Crazy patchwork box 22

8 Shoe sweeteners 26

9 Chatelaine 32

10 Brooch cushion 34

11 Tapestry box-lid 35

12 Crewel-work candlescreen 38

13 Embroidered towel edging 44

14 Oven cloth 45

15 Tea cosy 46

16 Pansy tray cloth 55

17 Heart of roses cushion 56

18 Flower-trellis cushion 60

19 Smocked cushion 62

20 Photo frame mat 65

21 Writing box 68

22 Notebook cover 69

23 Miniature garden scenes 71

The stitches 73

Handy hints 77

Suppliers 79

Index 80

Introduction

Garden plants and flowers have from the beginning inspired artists and craftspeople throughout the world. They have provided the basis for designs in clothing and pottery, household goods and personal accessories, precious metals and jewels, leather, clay and fabric and countless other art and craft materials.

For centuries embroiderers have interpreted in stitch and thread the flowers and vegetables, herbs, insects, birds and animals which they found within their gardens. Ingenious working methods were developed at various times, including the three-dimensional stumpwork of the early seventeenth century and the glorious folded, ruched and gathered appliqué flowers found on many nineteenth century Baltimore style quilts.

Just as the styles of embroidery have changed through the ages, so have the gardens which inspired many of their subjects. In recent times the traditional cottage garden has once again found favour as we look back nostalgically on a gentler age and seek to re-create the romance of the Victorian era. Century-old cottages are being lovingly restored, the recreation of their original gardens seen as important as the architecture. Old-fashioned crafts such as folk art painting, stencilling and découpage are being revived to complement the country style while gardeners are growing their own fruit and vegetables, often using traditional organic methods rather than the modern chemically-based fertilisers and pesticides.

Cottage gardens originally developed very haphazardly, as poor folk struggled to raise a few vegetables to feed their families. Into their little plots, other plants such as herbs were introduced for their medicinal properties, and wild plants were also tolerated if they were of use. Flowers were grown both for their perfume and for their attractiveness to bees, whose honey was also a valuable garden product. Chickens were kept to supply the family with eggs, and to add manure to the soil. For many people in the days before the Industrial Revolution the cottage garden provided many of life's necessities.

The early settlers who came to Australia carried on this system, bringing with them plants and livestock to start their new lives. To the traditional gardens of the British cottager they gradually added native species as well as plants from other parts of the world with similar climates. Subsequent migrants from other countries brought with them their own favourite plants, and thus the Australian cottage garden began to differ greatly from that of the British.

Cottage gardens were a very popular subject for embroidery through the 1930s to the 1950s. Stamped linens and iron-on transfer designs were easily obtained; magazines carried patterns for doilies and runners, tablecloths and cushion covers, adorned with pictures of brightly coloured hollyhocks and daisies. The Crinoline Lady, her features obscured by a poke bonnet, often presided over this floral abundance, surrounded by bluebirds and butterflies.

Certainly gardens provided just as much inspiration to the creative embroiderers of the following decades, but the call to 'do your own thing' saw realistic interpretations of plants and flowers give way to bold abstractions and complex patterns.

Now, in the 1990s, thanks to the work of many Australian embroiderers including Heather Joynes, Diana Lampe, Jenny Bradford and Elizabeth Moir, we are seeing a revival of old embroidery techniques in a new and stimulating way. Teachers are delighting in guiding the efforts of younger pupils who were never taught at school, as well as older embroiderers who are happily reviving their long neglected skills. We have available to us a wide range of wonderful materials; moirés and damasks, linens and brocades, as well as a bewildering assortment of threads and ribbons, beads and other embellishments. We can continue the traditions of generations of needleworkers by using them to interpret our gardens for our own pleasure and that of generations to come.

1 *Wisteria shadow box* *Illustrated on page 17*

MATERIALS

shadow box kit: pre-cut cardboard pieces
40 cm x 115 cm (16" x 45") beige linen-look fabric
40 cm x 30 cm (16" x 12") Shapewell woven interfacing
Appletons Crewel Wool, 1 skein each:
flame red 201*
iron grey 961
putty groundings 981
DMC Stranded Cotton, 1 skein each:

white	old gold 680
ecru	yellow 725
purple 208	baby pink 818
powder blue 341	very dark avocado 934
dark green 520	dark avocado 936
mid green 522	medium avocado 937
light green 524	pine green 3364
moss green 581	pale mauve 3689

DMC Pearl Cotton No. 5, 1 skein purple 208
craft glue
15 cm (6") No.1 piping cord for hanging loop

* Appletons 201, despite being the lowest number in the Flame Red colour range, is actually a warm beige shade.

1. Cut a rectangle 40 cm x 30 cm (16" x 12") from the linen-type fabric to prepare the front panel of the shadow box.
2. Trace the pattern for the box front directly onto the piece of Shapewell, using an HB lead pencil. With the pattern side facing up, and the wrong sides of the materials together, tack the interfacing onto the linen-look fabric, stitching around the outer edges, the arched opening and the lines of the wisteria stems, conifer and paving slabs.
3. Mount the interfaced section of fabric into a rectangular embroidery frame with the linen side uppermost. Thread a large-eyed needle with 3 strands of one shade of the crewel wool and bring it through from the back to the front of the fabric at lower point A, leaving a tail of about 2 cm (¾") on the wrong side. Repeat with the other two shades of wool, at lower points B and C, then stitch the ends securely to the Shapewell using matching sewing cotton and keeping the threads as flat as possible on the back of the work. Do not stitch through the linen fabric.
4. Divide the strands of wools into 3 stem groups, each a mixture of the different shades of wool. Lightly twist each in turn to make a cord, pinning the ends to the fabric as each one is finished. Twine the 3 cords through each other before stitching in turn onto the background fabric, from the base to the top left-hand corner, following the tacking lines. Using beige sewing cotton, lightly catch-stitch each cord invisibly in place through the thickness of the threads. Stems A and B branch at this point, gently unravel the strands of wool, divide in half, and re-twist. Continue to catch the stems in place as before across the top of the arch. Finish the end of each stem by threading the strands of wool through to the wrong side and sewing them to the Shapewell for about 2 cm (¾"). Cut off excess wool and remove the tacking thread from the stem lines.
5. Using 6 strands of cotton, embroider fly stitch leaves randomly through the canopy of the wisteria in the two shades of green, 936 and 3364. Overlap stitches, and position them so that the arms of the stitches point away from the stems of the plant. Keep the stitching within the lines tacked around the edge and the archway on the design.

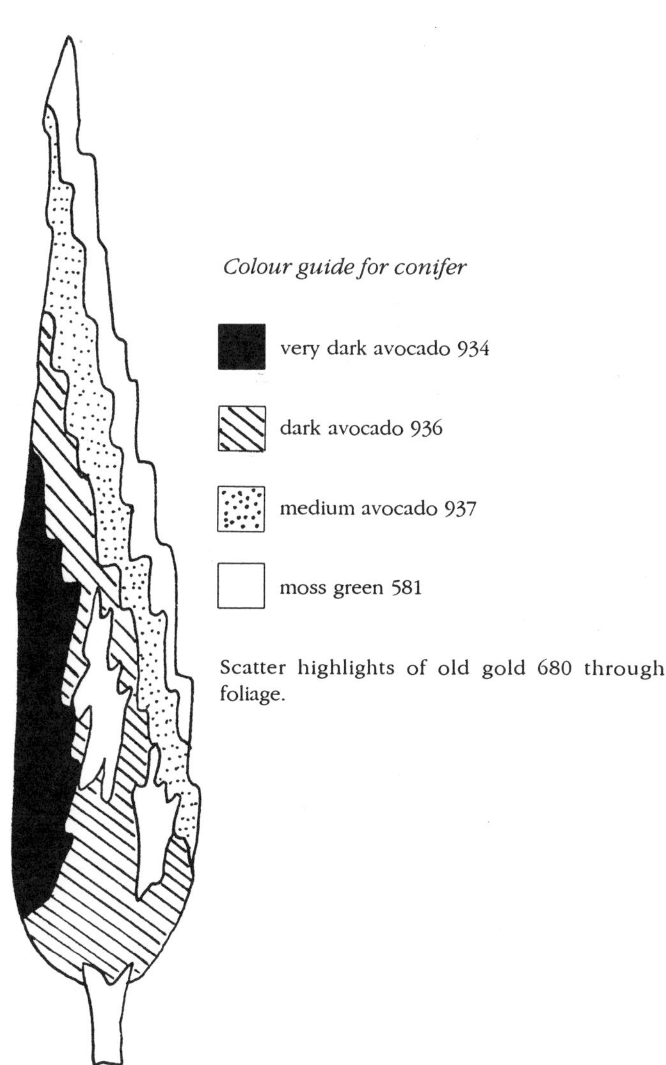

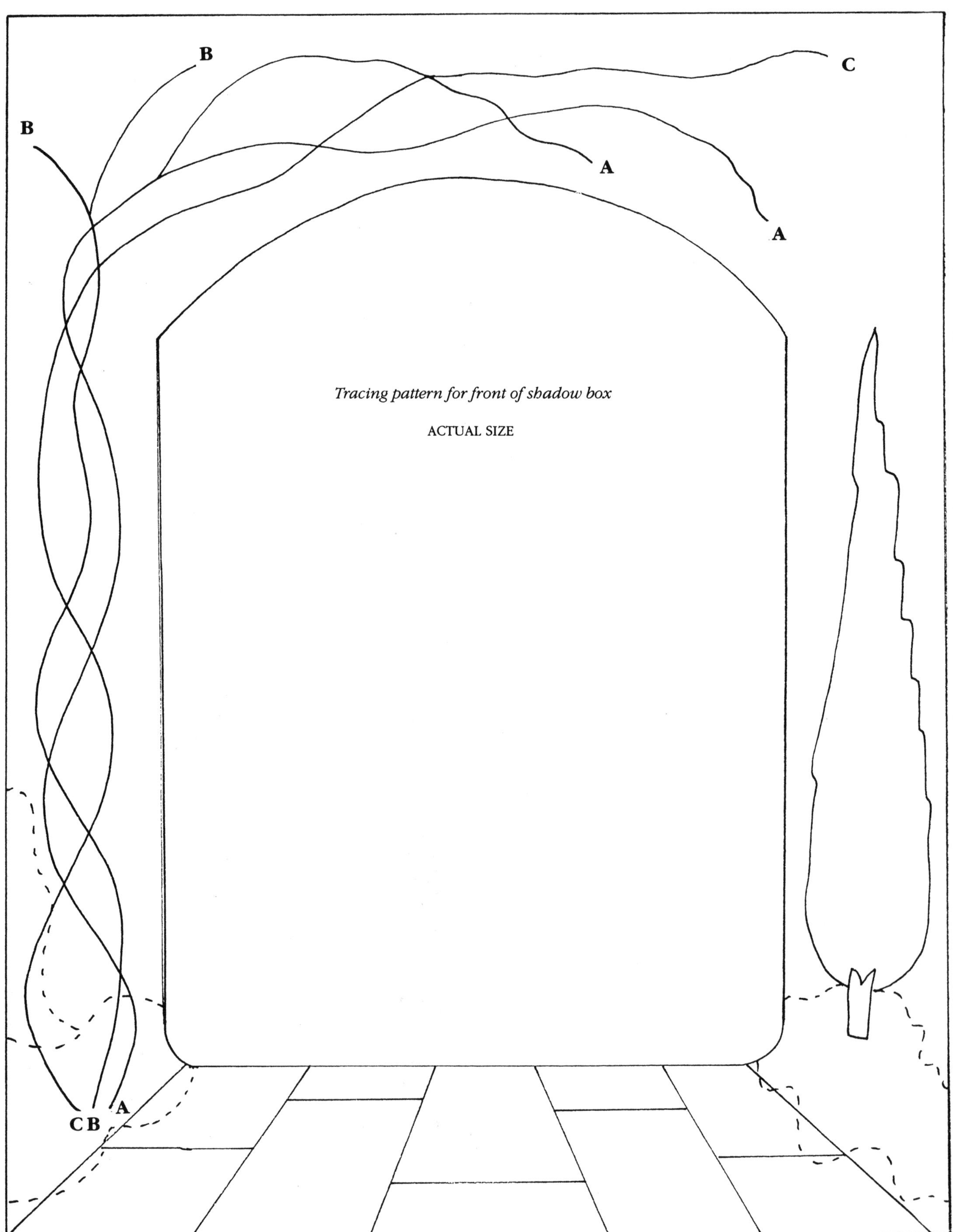
B
C
B
A
A
Tracing pattern for front of shadow box
ACTUAL SIZE
A
C B

6. Using 2 strands of mauve-purple pearl cotton 208, work French and bullion stitch knots through the canopy of the wisteria, singly and in small groups, to represent the flowers. Repeat this step using 3 strands of powder blue stranded cotton 341.
7. Using 2 strands of crewel wool iron grey 961, back stitch along the marked lines to represent paving slabs. Remove the tacking stitches.
8. Embroider the plants in the bottom left-hand corner. Work feather stitch for the fern, using 6 strands of green 936. The star-flower foliage consists of 8-wrap bullion knots in greens 520 and 522. Fill the area with randomly placed stitches, and finish by embroidering the flowers over the top of the foliage. The petals are straight stitches in 6 strands of white cotton, with French knot centres embroidered in 3 strands of yellow 725.
9. Embroider the conifer on the right-hand side of the arch in straight stitch. Use 6 strands of cotton throughout. Start with the trunk, using brown 680, and follow the colour guide to shade the colours, working upwards with stitches lying at a slight angle towards the edges and tapering to a rounded point at the top. When complete, remove the tacking stitches.
10. The clump of pinks at the base of the tree is worked in the same way as the white star flowers in the left-hand corner. The foliage consists of groups of 3 fly stitches in 6 strands of greens 522 and 524. The flowers are French knots using 6 strands of cotton, worked in ecru and pinks 818 and 3689.
11. When the embroidery is finished, remove it from the frame and place face down on a soft towel. Press lightly on the wrong side. Using a pair of sharp-pointed scissors, trim the *Shapewell only* back to the tacked lines. Following the manufacturer's instructions, mount the panel on the front section of the shadow box, aligning the tacked lines around the outside and the inner arch with the edges of the card. Remove the tacking threads after gluing the fabric in place.
12. Cover the other shadow box components with the remaining linen-look fabric. Assemble the box, and glue the completed embroidered section to the front edges.

2 *Calico mouse sachet*

Illustrated on page 18

MATERIALS

20 cm x 50 cm (8" x 20") cream calico (fabric 1)
17 cm x 13 cm (6¾" x 5") contrast fabric (fabric 2)
2 black wooden beads, 5 mm (3/16") diameter
80 cm (32") strong linen thread
15 cm (6") ribbon 7 mm (¼") wide
polyester fibrefill
small amount of potpourri or lavender
20 cm (8") ribbon 3 mm (1/8") wide
6 cm x 4 cm (2½" x 1½") thin card
DMC Stranded Cottons, 1 skein each:

dark pink 223	powder blue 341
medium pink 224	green 523
light pink 225	

1. Trace patterns A, B C and D and transfer them onto the calico as shown in the calico layout diagram. Cut one base insert from the thin card using pattern E.
2. Embroider the motifs following the placement and stitch diagram. When completed, press embroidery lightly on the wrong side.
3. Cut out the pieces around the marked lines. Seam allowance of 1 cm (3/8") is included.
4. With right sides together, join the two side sections (A) together along their curved edges.
5. With right sides facing, join piece D to the straight edges of the A sections. Turn the resulting cone shape to the right side and stuff with a mixture of fibrefill and potpourri. Turn in seam allowance around the bottom edges and sew one end of the 3 mm (1/8") ribbon to the inside back seam of the body.
6. Cover the card shape for the base insert with fabric piece B and slip stitch in place around the bottom edge of the cone shape, inserting extra stuffing as needed. Leave the long end of the narrow ribbon hanging out to form the mouse's tail.
7. Sew contrast fabric ear pieces to calico ear pieces around curved edges, right sides together. Turn to the right side and press flat. Tuck the raw edges to the inside and slip stitch along seam, pulling the stitches tightly so that the edges gather slightly. Sew the ears in position either side of the head on the marked lines, with the contrast fabric facing forward.
8. With doubled thread run a line of gathering stitches for the neckline along the marked line across the front section. Pull up slightly and finish off firmly with a couple of small back stitches. Sew a bow made from the 7 mm (¼") ribbon to the centre front over this line of stitching.
9. Sew the black beads over the eye dots marked on each

Tracing patterns

1 cm (3/8") seam allowance included

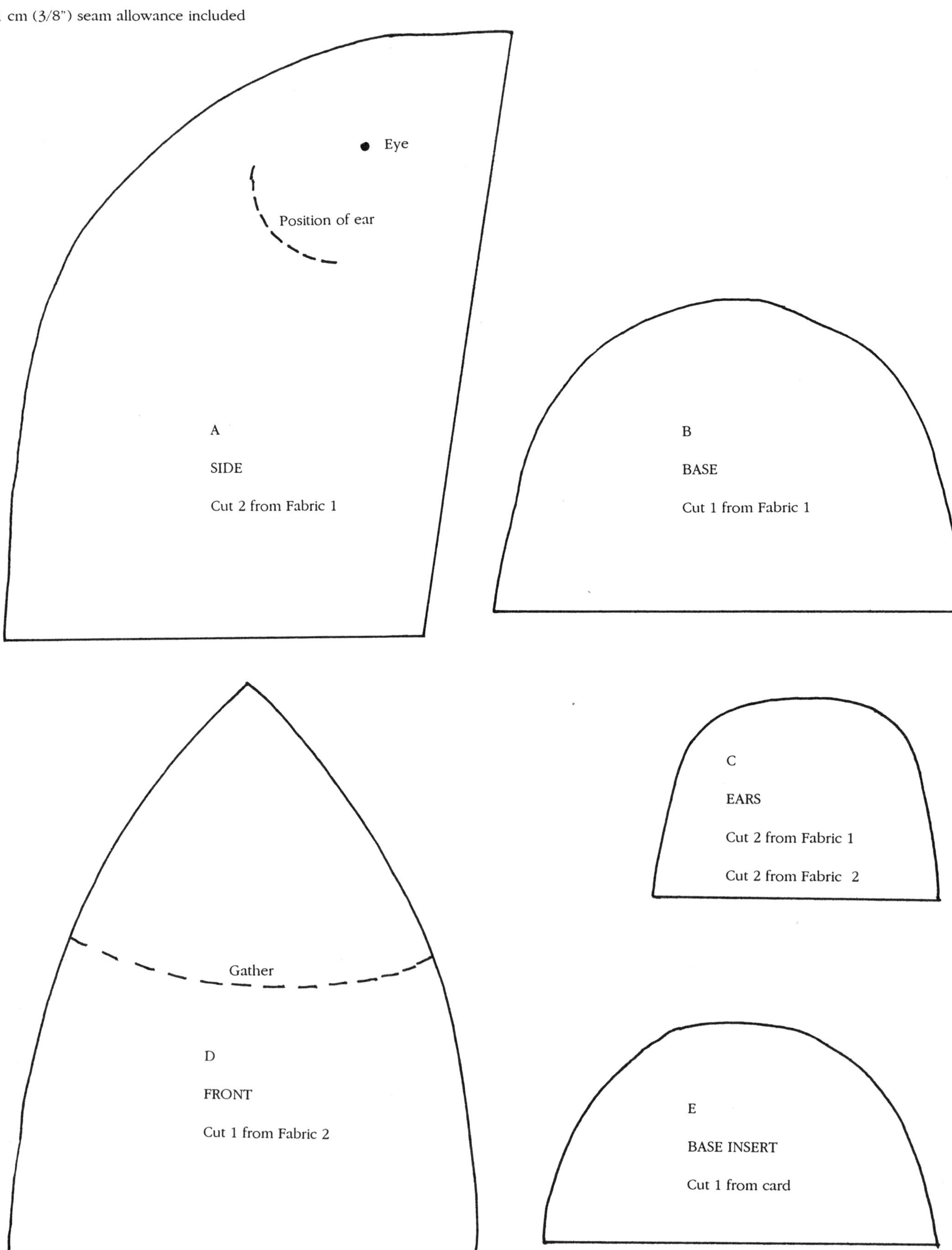

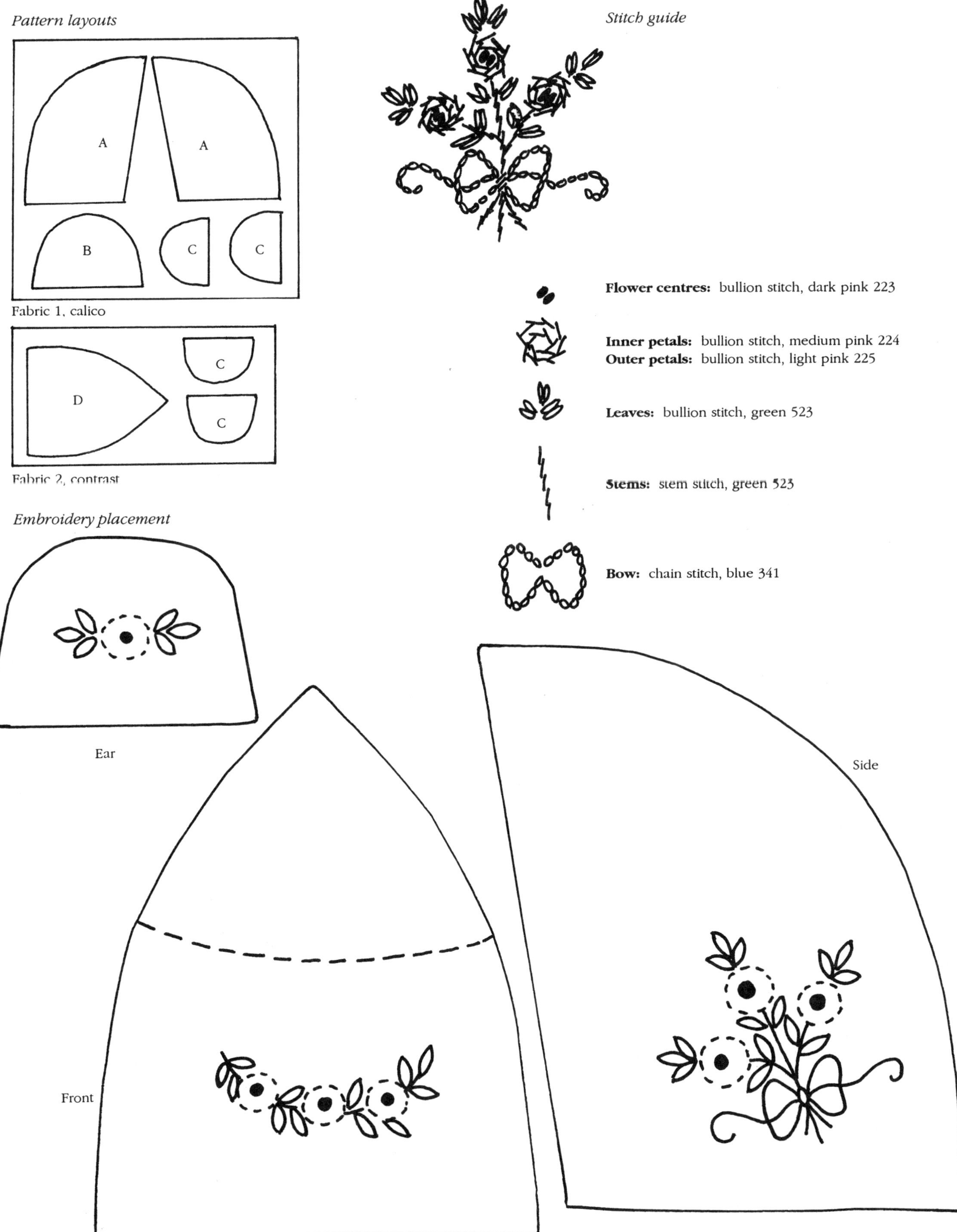
Pattern layouts
A
A
B
C
C
Fabric 1, calico
C
D
C
Fabric 2, contrast
Embroidery placement
Ear
Front
Side
Stitch guide
Flower centres: bullion stitch, dark pink 223
Inner petals: bullion stitch, medium pink 224
Outer petals: bullion stitch, light pink 225
Leaves: bullion stitch, green 523
Stems: stem stitch, green 523
Bow: chain stitch, blue 341

side of the head, pulling the thread tightly to indent them slightly. Fasten off the thread securely.

10. Fold the linen thread into 6 and tie an overhand knot about 5 cm (2") from one end. Thread the remaining ends through the dots marked on the nose, using a large needle. Pull tightly, then make a second overhand knot at the other side to secure. Cut the loops and trim the ends, fanning them out to make the whiskers.

Variation: Make both the front and the inside of the mouse's ears from a contrasting plain or print fabric, omitting the embroidery.

3 *Sweet pea pillowcase* *Illustrated on page 27*

MATERIALS

DMC Stranded Cotton, 1 skein each:

dark lilac 209	medium grass green 733
medium lilac 210	light grass green 734
pale lilac 211	medium salmon pink 776
medium powder blue 341	dark powder blue 794
dark sugar pink 603	light salmon pink 3689
medium sugar pink 604	dark salmon pink 3733
light sugar pink 605	light powder blue 3747
dark grass green 732	

80 cm (32") white cotton or linen fabric 115 cm (45") wide
1 m (39") white tape lace edging 14 cm (5½") wide

1. From the white fabric cut a piece 75 cm x 46 cm (29½" x 18") for the back of the pillowcase. For the front panel cut a piece 75 cm x 60 cm (29½" x 24").

2. Trace the embroidery pattern and transfer it to the top right-hand corner of the larger piece of fabric, 8 cm (3½") down from the raw edges at the top and 22 cm (8¾") in from the right-hand side.

3. Using 3 strands of thread for all embroidery, work the design in the stitches and colours shown in stitch diagram 1.

4. When the embroidery is complete, lightly press the work on the wrong side before making up the pillowcase.

5. Finish one short edge of the back panel of the pillowcase with a double hem 2.5 cm (1") wide.

6. Turn in a narrow double hem on the short edge of the embroidered panel closest to the embroidery.

7. Place the embroidered panel right side up and position the back of the pillowcase on top of it, right side down, with the raw edges matching. Turn the excess length of the embroidered piece over the end of the plain section as shown in the assembly diagram and pin in place through all layers of fabric.

8. Seam the two sections of the pillowcase together around the three unfinished edges. Turn to the right side. Hand stitch the tape lace trim to the edges of the opening, seaming the ends together at the bottom edge of the pillowcase.

Note: When making a matching pair, reverse the design for the second pillowcase.

Tracing pattern

ACTUAL SIZE

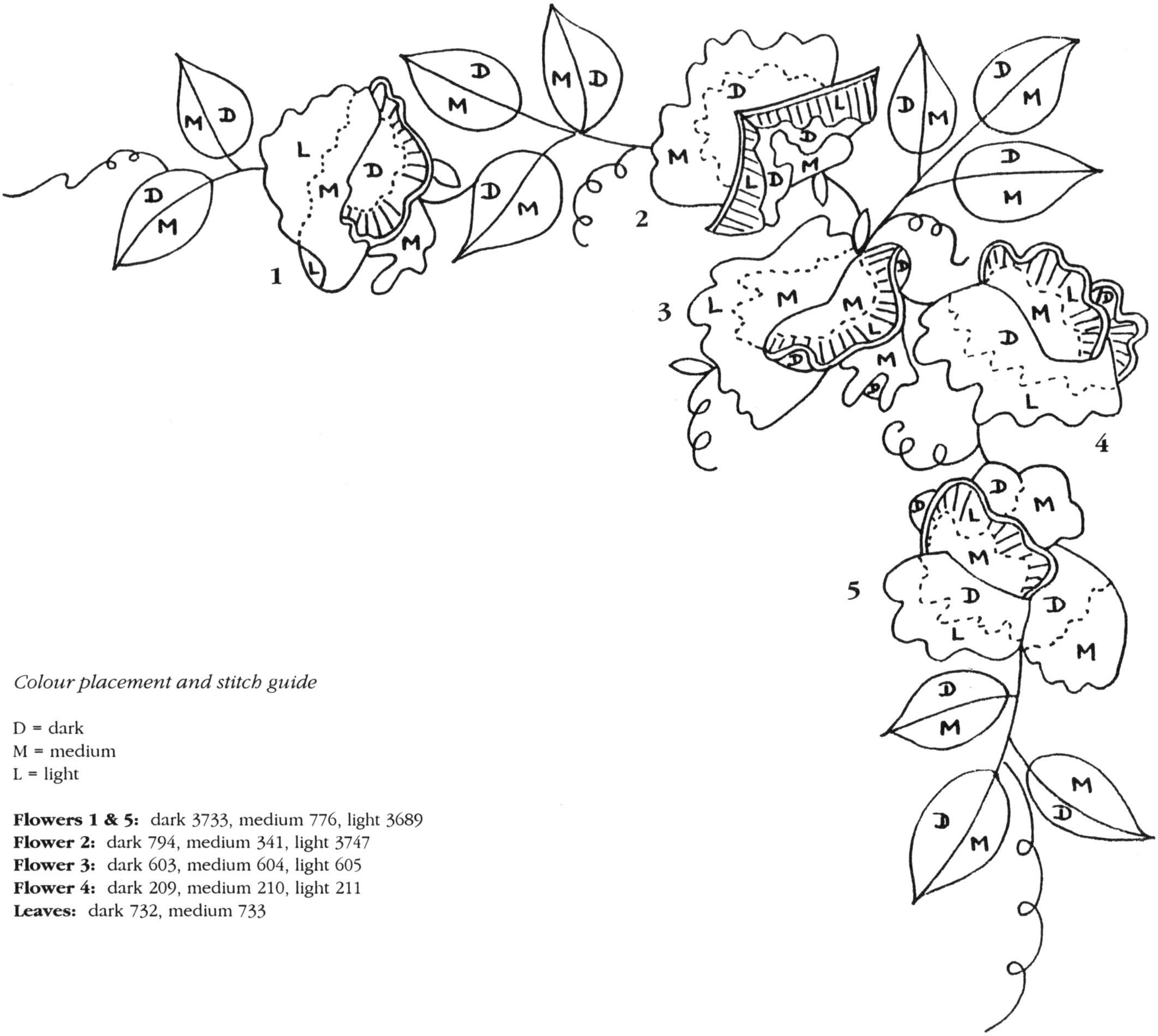

Colour placement and stitch guide

D = dark
M = medium
L = light

Flowers 1 & 5: dark 3733, medium 776, light 3689
Flower 2: dark 794, medium 341, light 3747
Flower 3: dark 603, medium 604, light 605
Flower 4: dark 209, medium 210, light 211
Leaves: dark 732, medium 733

Tendrils: split stitch, light green 734

Large leaves: satin stitch, greens 732 and 733

Flower petals: long & short stitch, in colours indicated on colour key chart (*Dotted line indicates shades merging*)

Flower petals: buttonhole stitch, in colours indicated on colour key chart (*Dotted line indicates shades merging*)

Small leaves: fishbone stitch, dark green 732

Stems: stem stitch, light green 734

Assembling pillowcase

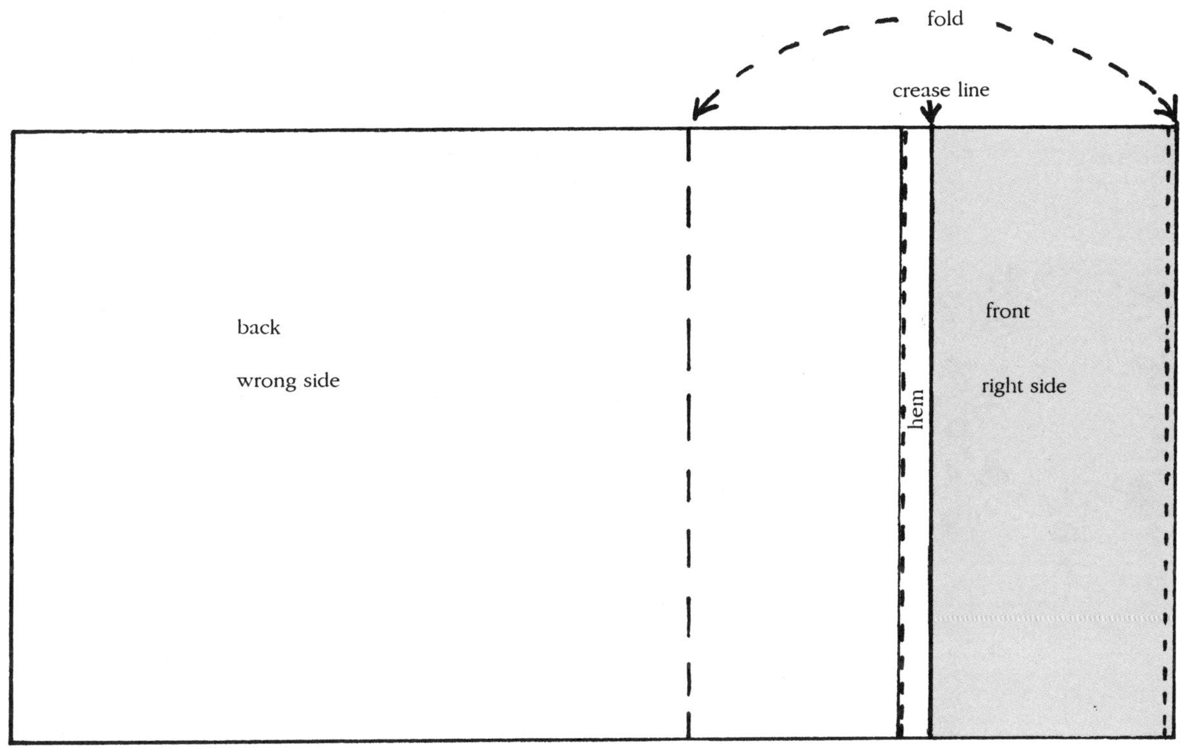

4 *Rose and initial crystal jar lid*

Illustrated on page 28

MATERIALS

15 cm (6") square dark powder blue silk
10 cm (4") burgundy silk ribbon 5 mm (2") wide
Madeira Glamour No. 8 thread, 1 reel gold 2424
Madeira silk thread, 1 packet each:
 pale pink 0502
 medium pink 0503
 dark rose 0812
 dark emerald 1312
10 cm (4") square quilt wadding
Framecraft crystal jar with 7.5 cm (3") diameter lid

1. Trace the design from the pattern diagram. Centre the design over the required initial from the alphabet guide and trace that too.
2. Transfer the design to the centre of the square of silk fabric, and stretch the material in a 10 cm (4") embroidery hoop before beginning to sew.
3. Using one strand of thread for all embroidery, work the design following the stitch and colour guide. Start with the buds and flowers, then embroider the stems and leaves.
4. Work the initial in back stitch using the gold thread, starting where you would if you were writing the letter with a pen. The line of back stitch should cross over itself where necessary, just as an inked line would.
5. Using a needle with an eye large enough to take the full width of the ribbon, thread the silk ribbon through the marked points at the base of the design, leaving both ends at the front of the work. Pull the ribbon through gently until the ends are of equal length, then tie them in a bow. Trim the ends.
6. Using the card supplied with the jar lid as a pattern, cut out the embroidered design, leaving a margin of 1.5 cm (5/8") fabric all around. Lightly glue the card to the centre of the square of wadding, and trim off the excess.
7. Centre the embroidery over the circle of wadding-covered card and glue the turnings neatly to the back. Mount the embroidery into the rim of the lid following the manufacturer's instructions.

Tracing pattern

ACTUAL SIZE

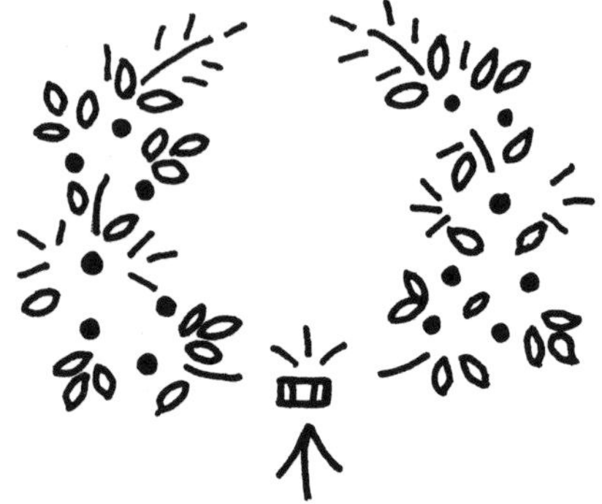

Colour placement and stitch guide

Alphabet tracing pattern

ACTUAL SIZE

Buds: bullion stitch, medium pink 0503
Sepals: fly stitch, dark emerald 1312

Stems: stem stitch, dark emerald 1312

Leaves: lazy daisy, dark emerald 1312

Roses
centres: bullion stitch, dark rose 0812
inner petals: bullion stitch, medium pink 0503
outer petals: bullion stitch, pale pink 0502

Ribbon placement

Initial: back stitch, gold 2424

5 *Topiary rose tree*

Illustrated on page 29

MATERIALS

terracotta half pot 4 cm (1½") high
background fabric (silk or brocade type), 26 cm x 21 cm (10¾" x 8¾")
12 cm (4¾") square calico
small amount fibrefill
5 cm (2") square brown velvet
10 cm (4") piping cord No.1
3 mm (3/32") silk ribbon, 2 m (2¼ yds) each:

medium pink	dark green
light pink	medium green
white	light green

1 packet 2 mm (1/16") white pearl beads
1 reel Kreinik Balger #8 braid 002 HL Gold
DMC Stranded Cotton, 1 skein each:
baby pink 818
dark brown 898
cream sewing thread
picture frame with glass removed, inside measurement 16.5 cm x 11.5 cm (6½" x 4½")

1. Trace the pattern and transfer it to the centre of the background fabric. Use a crewel needle for all embroidery except where indicated.
2. Position the piping cord on top of the fabric, over the line of the tree trunk, and couch in place with 3 strands of brown stranded cotton, using horizontal stitches spaced about 5 mm (3/16") apart.
3. Cover the cord with a raised stem band; work parallel lines of stem stitch over the piping cord, using the couching stitches as a foundation, in 6 strands of brown stranded cotton. Use a tapestry needle to avoid splitting the threads, and pack the rows together tightly until the cord is no longer visible beneath them.
4. With green ribbons in random choice of shades, work pairs of lazy daisy leaves around the outside edge of the top circle as shown, covering each of the marked lines on the pattern.
5. Trace the pattern for the top section and transfer it to the centre of the square of calico. Mount the fabric in a small embroidery hoop.

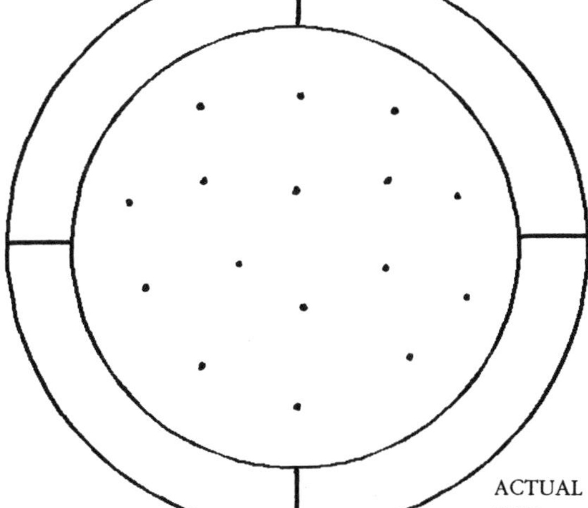

Tracing pattern for top section

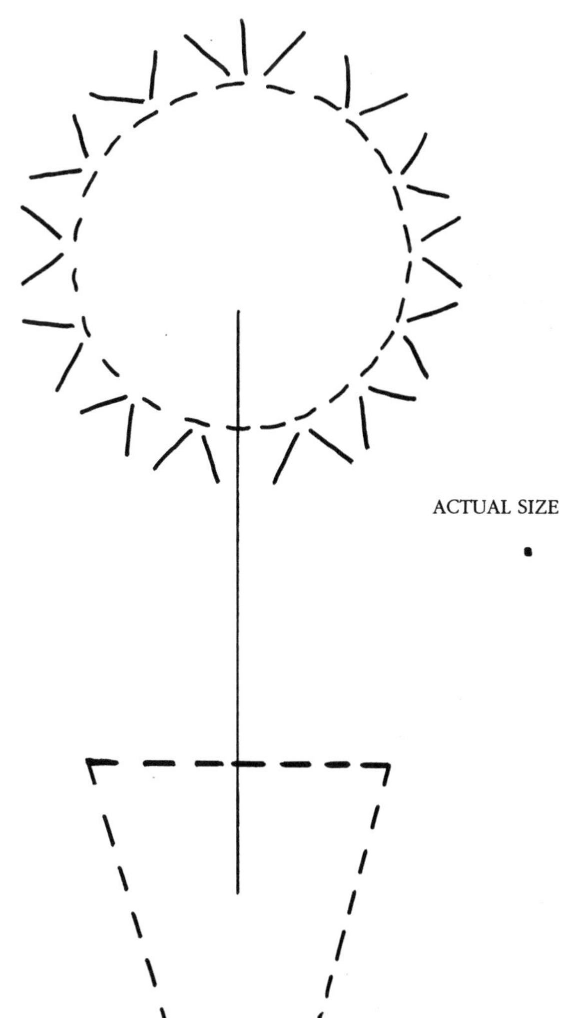

Tracing pattern for outline

6. Using 2 strands of stranded cotton in baby pink 818, work 5 straight stitches radiating from each of the marked dots. Change to a tapestry needle and work the spider's web roses on each set of foundation stitches, using the pink and white silk ribbons.

7. Fill any gaps between the roses with lazy daisy stitch leaves in green ribbon and add a random scattering of pearl beads as highlights.

8. Trim the excess fabric around the circle to within 15 mm (5/8") of the stitching and fold the raw edges to the back. Pin in place over the marked circle on the main embroidery.

9. Slip stitch three-quarters of the embroidered circle in place using sewing cotton to match the background fabric. Insert enough fibrefill through the opening to gently round out the shape of the tree top and raise it from the background. Slip stitch the remaining section of the circle in place

10. Work more green leaves in lazy daisy stitch to fill the gaps around the edge of the padded circle, allowing them to spill from the appliqué onto the background fabric.

11. Using one strand of gold thread, work an interlocking star stitch at each of the dots marked around the tree on the background fabric.

12. Mount the embroidery onto a piece of card ready for framing, allowing enough space at the bottom to position the half pot.

13. Using a clear craft glue, fix the half pot to the base of the tree trunk so that it covers the pattern lines. Trim the brown velvet to fit inside the pot, hiding the base of the tree trunk, and glue the edges to the inside of the pot and the background fabric, with the raw edges to the inside.

14. Make a twisted cord with tasselled ends from three 1 m (39") lengths of gold thread and pass it from left to right behind the tree trunk, halfway between the pot and the rose embroidery. Use a large needle or a bodkin, and do not pierce the background fabric. Adjust the cord until the ends are of equal length, and tie them in a bow around the tree trunk. The ends can be lightly glued in place if desired.

15. Position the completed embroidery in the frame.

Bonus design

Wisteria shadow box (page 5) complements tiny treasures

Delightful calico mouse sachets (page 7) can be filled with lavender or potpourri

Oval-shaped crazy patchwork box (page 22) is used here to store notepaper

6 *Cross-stitch sampler*

Illustrated on page 30

MATERIALS

45 cm x 50 cm (18" x 20") natural linen-colour Aida cloth, 14 threads per 2.5 cm (1")

Anchor Stranded Cotton, 1 skein each:

- white 1
- dark purple 102
- light purple 109
- blue 118
- medium grass green 267
- dark grass green 269
- cream 275
- beige 276
- light yellow 295
- mid yellow 298
- dark yellow 306
- gold 308
- ginger 347
- buttermilk 361
- dark brown 382
- mid blue green 877
- dark blue green 879
- dark olive green 905
- cinnamon 914

Minnamurra Threads Stranded Cotton, 1 skein each:

- blue/purple MT10
- pink/mauve MT30
- mauve/gold MT110
- pink/grey MT130
- green/yellow MT180
- green/apricot MT210
- green/blue MT220

1. Overlock the raw edges of the Aida cloth to prevent fraying. Mark the centre lines in both directions with tacking thread in a contrasting colour.

2. Following the chart, on which each square represents one cross-stitch, work the embroidery using the thread colours as shown. All cross-stitches are worked with 3 strands of thread while the back-stitched lines are worked with 2 strands. When using the Minnamurra threads, work each stitch singly to retain their variegated effect.

3. When all the embroidery has been completed, remove the tacking threads and lightly press the sampler on the wrong side. Mount and frame as desired.

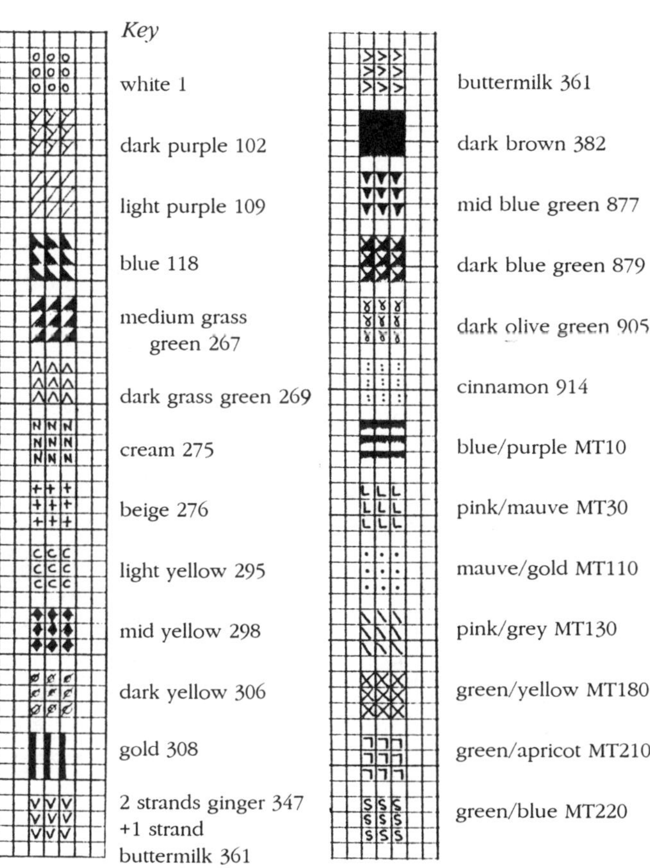

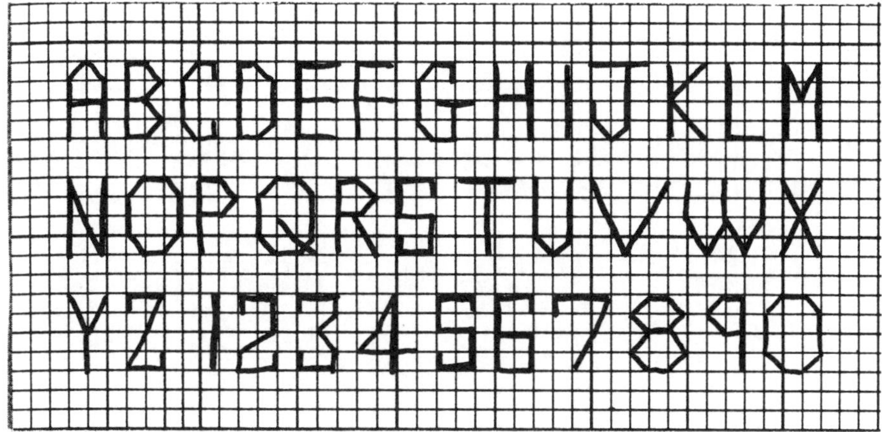

Alphabet chart

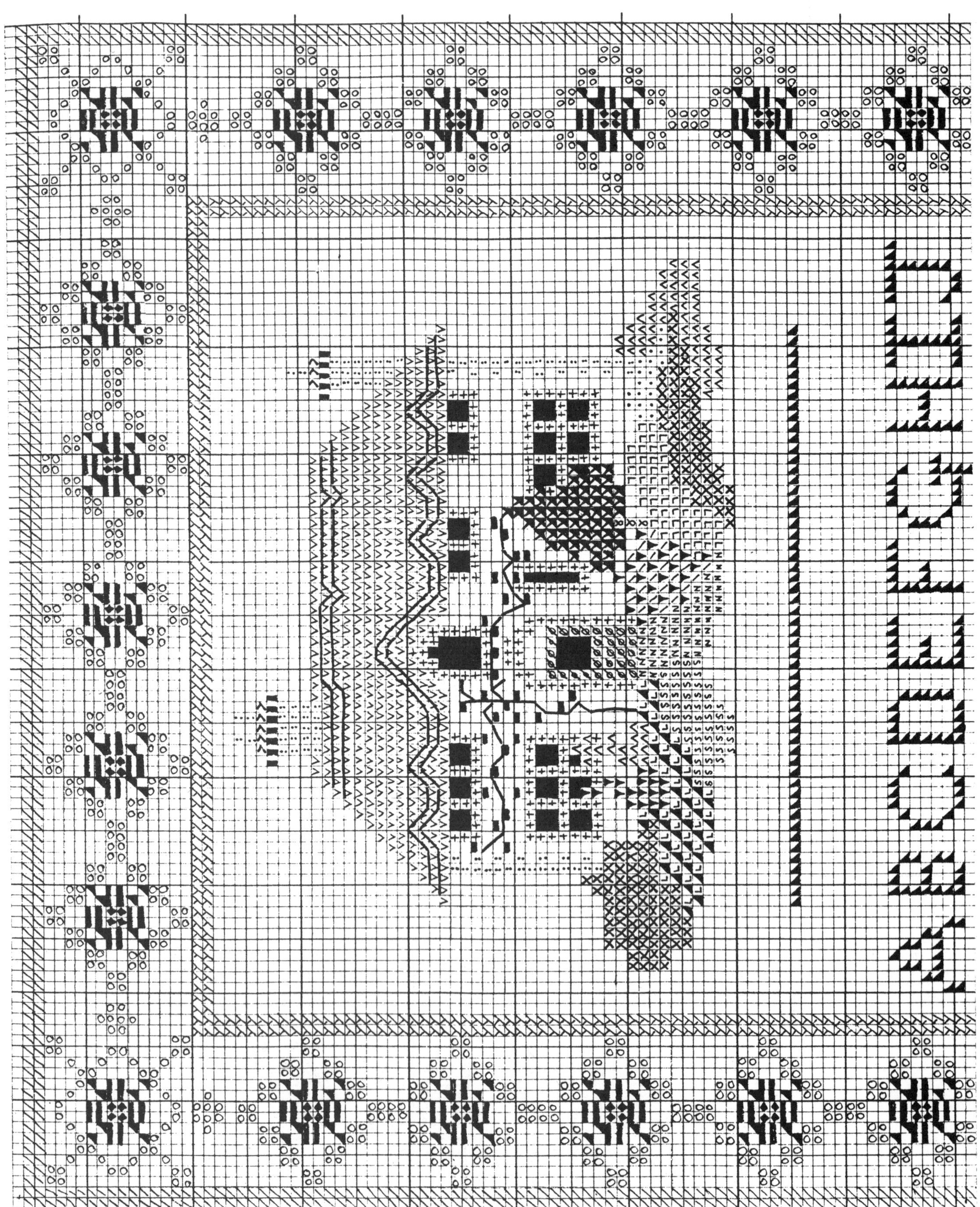

Cross-stitch sampler chart

each square represents one cross-stitch

7 *Crazy patchwork box*

Illustrated on page 18

MATERIALS

30 cm (12") square calico
30 cm (12") square burgundy silk
30 cm (12") square pale green silk
15 cm (6") square cream silk
matching sewing cottons
1 m (40") antique gold braid, 5 mm (3/16") wide
60 cm (24") antique gold braid, 25 mm (1") wide
30 cm (12") square wadding
craft glue
oval wooden box, 20.5 cm x 16.5 cm (8" x 6½")
folk art paints:
- gold
- burgundy

all-purpose sealer
crackle glaze
DMC Stranded Cottons, 1 skein each:

white	golden yellow 725
dark purple 209	olive green 732
medium purple 210	pale olive 734
light purple 211	light yellow 745
dark pink 223	very dark green 934
medium pink 224	light gold-brown 977
light pink 225	electric blue 996
sky blue 341	bright green 3346
grey green 504	mid green 3364
dark green 520	dark pink 3689
mid green 522	pale melon pink 3708
dark crimson 603	pale blue 3747
mid crimson 604	dark tan 3772
light crimson 605	light tan 3773

1. Trace the straight lines and outside oval from the master pattern and transfer onto the piece of calico.
2. Trace the motifs individually and transfer A to the cream silk, B, D and F to the burgundy silk and C, E and G to the pale green silk. Leave enough room between the motifs to cut out the shapes according to the master pattern, including a seam allowance of 1.5 cm (5/8").
3. Embroider the motifs, using the colours and stitches in the stitch guide, with 2 strands of stranded cotton.
4. Cut the master pattern tracing along the straight lines and use the sections as templates to cut out the motifs from the fabrics, leaving 1.5 cm (5/8") seam allowance around all the edges.
5. Centre patch A over the corresponding shape drawn on the calico and tack in place. Fold under the longest edge of patch B and position it over the shape marked on the calico, with the folded edge covering the seam allowance of patch A. Slip stitch in place using matching sewing thread.
6. Position the remaining patches in the same manner, working through them in alphabetical order. Turn over the edges which will cover the seam allowances of previously placed patches, and leave raw edges where they will in turn be covered by the adjoining pieces. Patch G will have both edges turned under. Stitch only along the straight edges, as far as the oval outline on the calico, and leave the curved edges free.
7. When all stitching is complete, remove tacking threads, then turn the work over and cut around the edge of the oval, *through the calico only*. Trim the edges of the silk patchwork to 1.5 cm (5/8") beyond the edge of the calico oval.
8. Stitch narrow braid in place by hand along all the straight seam lines, extending out to the edges of the oval.
9. Prepare the wooden box by painting it with folk art paints. Mix equal quantities of all-purpose sealer with gold and apply two coats of paint to the inside and outside of the box and to the inside of the lid. Let dry. Paint one coat of crackle glaze over the gold paint and allow to dry. Finish by painting the final coat in burgundy, using long sweeping brush strokes.
10. When the painted box is completely dry, glue wadding to the top of the lid. Trim to fit.
11. Centre the patchwork oval on top of the wadding and glue the edges down evenly around the sides of the lid. Trim away excess fabric.
12. Cover the raw edges of the fabric by gluing the 25 mm (1") gold braid around the edge of the lid.

Master tracing pattern

ACTUAL SIZE

A: Cornucopia
Left centre rose petal, buds on left side: satin stitch, mid crimson 604
Top left, middle right petals and bud: satin stitch, light crimson 605
Remaining petals, top bud: satin stitch, 1 strand each 605/white
Centre: French knots, light yellow 745
Leaves (use one green for each side): satin stitch, dark green 520, mid green 522, mid green 3364
Cornucopia outline: chain stitch, dark tan 3772
Cornucopia infill: trellis stitch, light tan 3773
Centre of rose: satin stitch, light yellow, 745
Right hand spray small buds: bullion stitch, mid crimson 604
Calyx: fly stitch, grey green 504
Stems: stem stitch, grey green 504

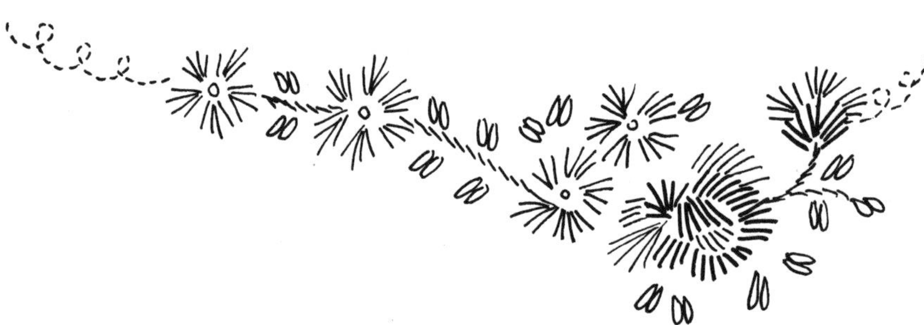

B: Long flower spray
Leaves: bullion stitch, dark green 520
Stems: stem stitch, dark green 520
Tendrils: back stitch, dark green 520
Centre and left side petals of rose: satin stitch, dark pink 223
Middle petals of rose, base of bud: satin stitch, medium pink 224
Outer petals of rose and bud: satin stitch, light pink 225
Open flower petals: satin stitch, sky blue 341
Flower centres: French knots, light yellow 745

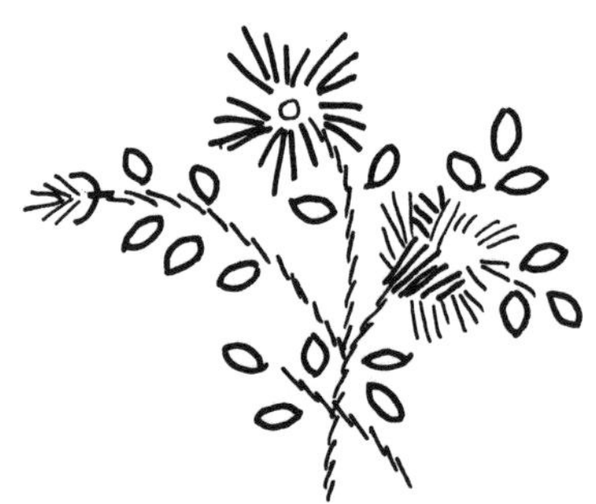

C: Small bouquet
Lower stem: stem stitch, very dark green 934
Main stem: stem stitch, mid green 3364
Lower leaves: lazy daisy, very dark green 934
Remaining leaves: lazy daisy, mid green 3364
Centre & left petals of rose & bud: satin stitch, dark crimson 603
Petals around centre of rose: satin stitch, mid crimson 604
Right hand rose petals: satin stitch, light crimson 605
Open flower: satin stitch, sky blue 341
Base of bud: fly stitch, very dark green 934
Centre of open flower: French knot, yellow 745

D: Water lily
Stems: stem stitch, dark green 520
Leaves: lazy daisy, dark green 520
Lower centre petal, 3rd side petals & middle centre, upper petal: satin stitch, dark purple 209
2nd side petals, lower centre petal & top outer petals: satin stitch, medium purple 210
Top centre petal, angled centre petals & lower side petals: satin stitch, light purple 211

E: Three-flower spray
Leaves: lazy daisy, bright green 3346
Stems: stem stitch, bright green 3346
Bow: back stitch, electric blue 996
Flower centres: French knots, golden yellow 725
Flowers: buttonhole stitch, 1 strand each 3747 & white

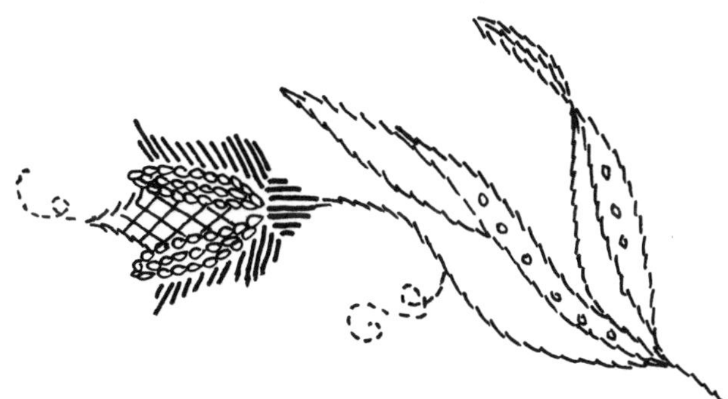

F: Tulip
Stem & lower leaf outlines: stem stitch, olive green 732
Leaf tips, top & tip of lower leaf: stem stitch, pale olive 734
Lower leaf fillings: French knots, olive green 732
Tendril off stem: back stitch, olive green 732
Tendril off flower: back stitch, pale olive 734
Base of flower: satin stitch, olive green 732
Outer petals: satin stitch, mid crimson 604
Inner petals: chain stitch, light crimson 605
Outline of centre petal: stem stitch, 1 strand each 605 & white
Filling of centre petal: trellis stitch, 1 strand each 605 & white

G: Grub rose spray
Stems: stem stitch, dark green 520
Leaves: lazy daisy, grey green 504
Bow: split stitch, light gold-brown 977
Outer petals: bullion stitch, pale melon pink 3708
Inner petals and buds: bullion stitch, dark pink 3689
Calyx at base of buds: fly stitch, dark green 520

8 *Shoe sweeteners*

Illustrated on page 39

MATERIALS

30 cm (12") ivory silk 115 cm (45") wide
Rajmahal Art Silk, 1 skein each:

- baby camel 45
- laurel green 65
- purple dusk 113
- bluebell 121
- dusky rose 241
- grape 243
- maidenhair 521
- damask rose 742
- melaleuca 802

70 cm (28") gold cord
polyester fibrefill
scoop of dried lavender or potpourri

1. Trace the pattern and transfer it twice onto the silk fabric.
2. Embroider the motifs onto the fabric following the stitch and colour placement guide. Use 2 strands of thread for all the stitchery.
3. When the embroidery is complete, press each piece gently on the wrong side.

Stitch and colour placement guide

Top flower
centre: satin stitch, grape 24
petals: satin stitch, damask rose 742

Upper leaves: lazy daisy, maidenhair 521, melaleuca 802

Rosebud petals:
bullion stitch, grape 24
calyx: fly stitch, melaleuca 802

Small flowers: French knots, purple dusk 113, bluebell 121

Stems: stem stitch, melaleuca 802
Leaves: lazy daisy, laurel green 65

Open flowers: lazy daisy, damask rose 742

Heart: chain stitch filling, baby camel 45

Ferns: feather stitch, melaleuca 802

Bottom flower
centre: satin stitch, grape 243
petals: satin stitch, dusky rose 241

Deep frills of fabric and lace finish the flower-trellis cushion (page 60) and the sweet pea pillowcase (page 10)

Detail of sweet pea pillowcase embroidery

Detail of flower trellis cushion

Flower-trimmed brooch cushion (page 34)

Bullion roses and gold thread adorn the rose and initial crystal jar lid (page 13)

Topiary rose tree (page 15) is beautifully set off by a heavy gold frame

Detail of embroidery

Cross-stitch sampler (page 19) features a rich border of stylised flowers

Tracing pattern

Pattern includes seam allowances of 1 cm (3/8") on sides and 5 mm (3/16") on scalloped top edge

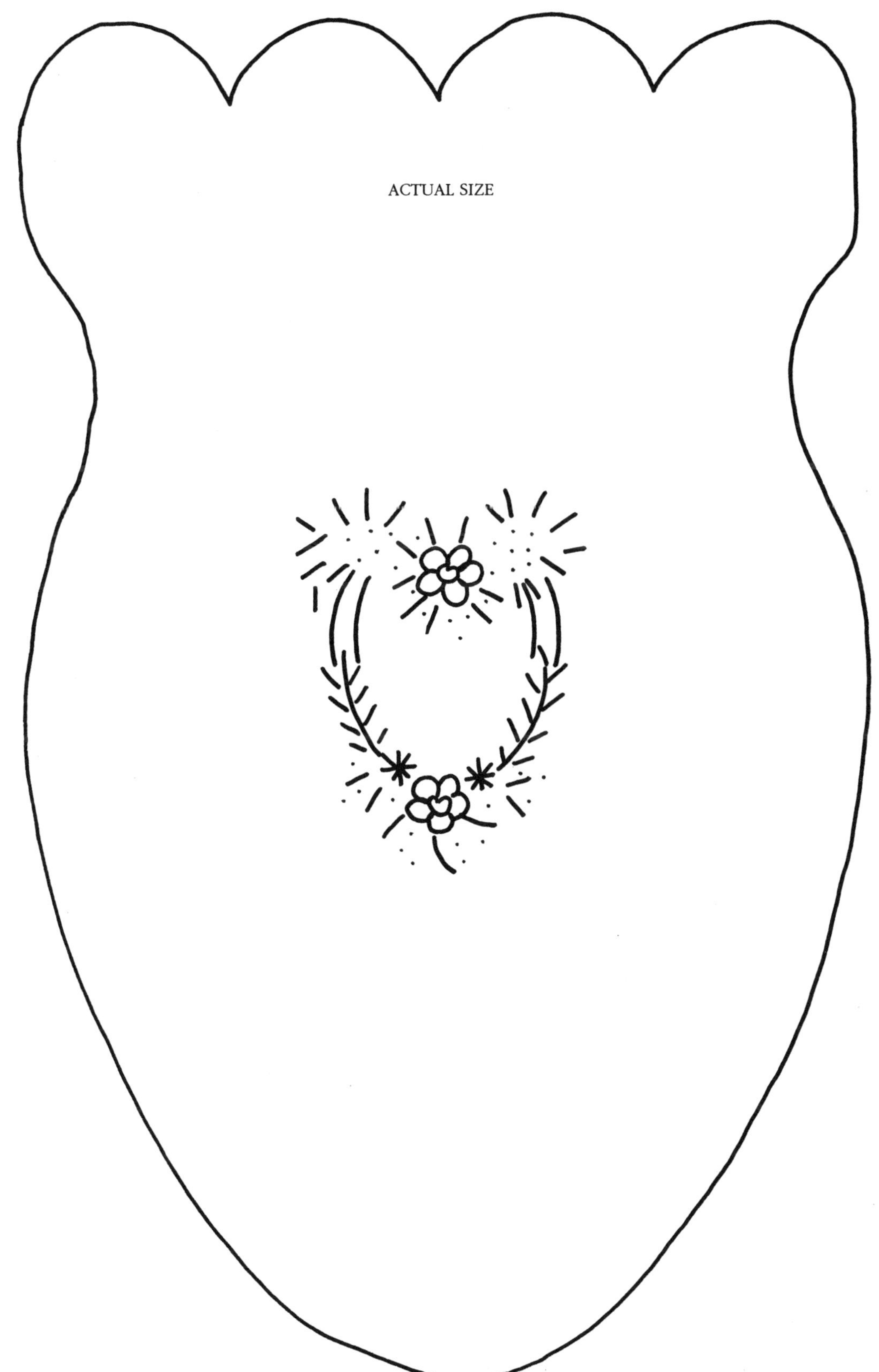

4. Cut out the two embroidered shapes. Using one of them as a pattern, cut out 2 more shapes from the remaining fabric.

5. With right sides together, sew one plain piece to each of the embroidered sections, leaving the short scalloped edges open.

6. From the remaining fabric, cut 4 pieces 15 cm x 7.5 cm (6" x 3") and seam together in pairs along their shorter sides. Finish one long edge of each band by turning under a narrow hem and top stitching.

7. Turn bands to the right side and slip inside the shoe sweeteners, right sides facing, matching the seams, and allowing the scalloped edges to rest just below the unfinished straight edge of each facing.

8. Following the line of the scallops, and taking a seam allowance of 5 mm (3/16"), join the facings to the shoe sweeteners. Trim seams and clip allowances before turning through to the right side. Finish the facings by top stitching around the scalloped edge on the right side.

9. Fill each of the shoe sweeteners with a mixture of fibrefill and dried lavender, to just cover the lower edge of the facing. Cut the gold braid in half and tie one piece firmly around the top of each insert, tucking the facing down into the filling and enclosing it as smoothly as possible. Tie the ends of the braid into bows.

9 Chatelaine

Illustrated on page 40

Tracing patterns (actual size)

Scissors case

Needle book

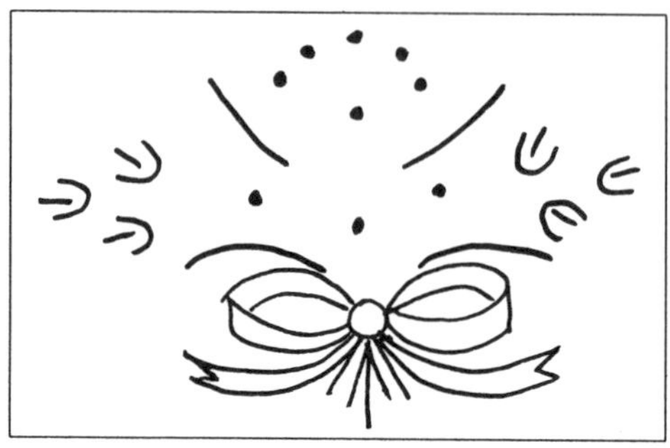

Thimble pod

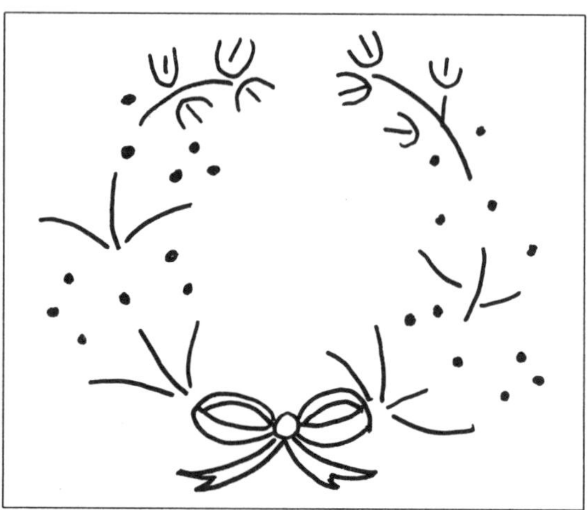

Pin wheel

MATERIALS

pre-cut cardboard chatelaine kit
15 cm (6") fabric 115 cm (45") wide
15 cm (6") lining fabric 115 cm (45") wide
15 cm x 50 cm (6" x 20") wadding
10 cm x 6.5 cm (4" x 2½") felt
1 m (40") cord
2 tassels, 4 cm (1½") long
Rajmahal silk threads, 1 skein each:

baby camel 45	cossack blue 122
white 96	barely pink 200
bluebell 121	petal pink 202

DMC Stranded Cotton, 1 skein:
fern green 522

1. Trace the patterns and transfer them to the fabric following the layout diagram. If you like, include an initial in the design for the pin wheel, traced from the alphabet on page 14.
2. Following the stitch and colour placement diagrams, embroider the designs onto the fabric. Use 2 strands of thread for all stitchery. It is easier to work all the embroidery before cutting out the individual sections.
3. Lightly press the finished embroidery on the wrong side, then cut out the sections, leaving a seam allowance of 1 cm (3/8") around the edges. Mount them over the pre-cut sections of card according to the manufacturer's instructions.
4. Finish the chatelaine by mounting the pieces on the length of cord, and sewing the tassels at the base of the scissors case and thimble pod.

Colour placement and stitch guide

Leaves: feather stitch,
DMC fern green 522

Rose buds
petals: bullion knots,
Rajmahal petal pink 202
stems: stem stitch,
DMC fern green 522
sepals: fly stitch,
DMC fern green 522

Roses
centres: bullion knots,
Rajmahal petal pink 202
inner petals: bullion knots,
Rajmahal barely pink 200
outer petals: bullion knots,
Rajmahal white 96

Small flowers: French knots,
Rajmahal bluebell 121

Bows: chain stitch,
Rajmahal cossack blue 122

Initial: chain stitch,
Rajmahal baby camel 45

Pattern layout

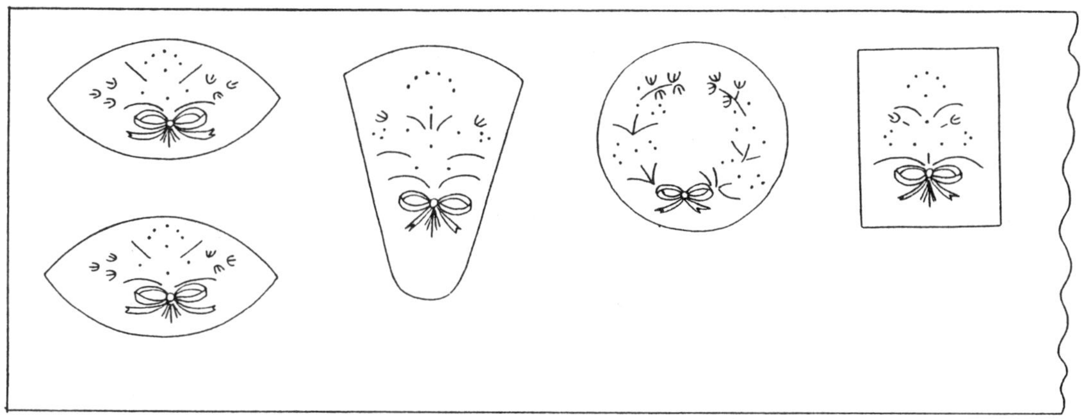

10 *Brooch cushion* *Illustrated on page 28*

MATERIALS

20 cm (8") ivory silk in a slub finish, 115 cm (45") wide
20 cm x 54 cm (8" x 21½") lightweight wadding
polyester fibrefill
15 cm x 30 cm (6" x 12") calico
1.5 m (60") cream braid 6 mm (¼") wide
40 cm (15¾") ivory silk-finish cord 10 mm (3/8") in diameter
1 packet 2 mm (1/16") diameter pearl beads
1.2 m (48") fine gauge wire
65 cm x 3 cm (26" x 1¼") ivory silk taffeta
Fray Stoppa
50 cm (20") ivory organdie ribbon 27 mm (1 1/16") wide
Ribbon Floss, gold
Anchor Stranded Cottons, 1 skein each:
greens 264, 265, 266, 267, 268

1. Cut two rectangles 19 cm x 25.5 cm (7½" x 10") from both the ivory slub silk and the thin wadding.
2. Trace the pattern for the brooch cushion and transfer it to the centre of one of the panels of silk. Tack the marked fabric onto one piece of wadding and mount into a 20 cm (8") embroidery hoop. Set the remaining pieces to one side.
3. Cut lengths of braid just slightly longer than the lines marked across the oval on the pattern, and pin them in place covering the markings. Work in each direction in turn. Slip stitch the braid in place using matching sewing cotton.
4. Using gold Ribbon Floss, embroider a French knot in the centre of each intersection, working through both thicknesses of braid, the foundation fabric and the wadding.
5. Trim the ends of the braid level with the outline of the oval. Cover the raw edges by slip stitching the ivory cord in place on the line of the oval, beginning and ending at the star-shaped markings. Flatten the ends of the cord by unravelling them for 1 cm (5/8") and stitching the individual strands down side by side.
6. Mount the strip of calico into a 10 cm (4") embroidery hoop, starting near one end of the fabric. Transfer the leaf pattern onto it three times, evenly spaced, with all motifs pointing in the same direction.
7. Embroider the leaves onto the calico in padded satin stitch. Use 2 strands of thread in 2 shades of green stranded cotton, one darker and one lighter, for each leaf. Mix and match the shades at random.
8. Cut a piece of wire 20 cm (8") long and position it along the centre line of the first leaf with one end of the wire resting at the tip. Using 2 strands of the darker green used for that leaf, couch the wire in place down the centre line of the leaf. Bend it at the base of the leaf, curving it back to follow the outside edge—see diagram. Couch the wire up to the tip, then bend it back again and couch down the other side of the leaf. Leave the end of the wire pointing

Tracing patterns

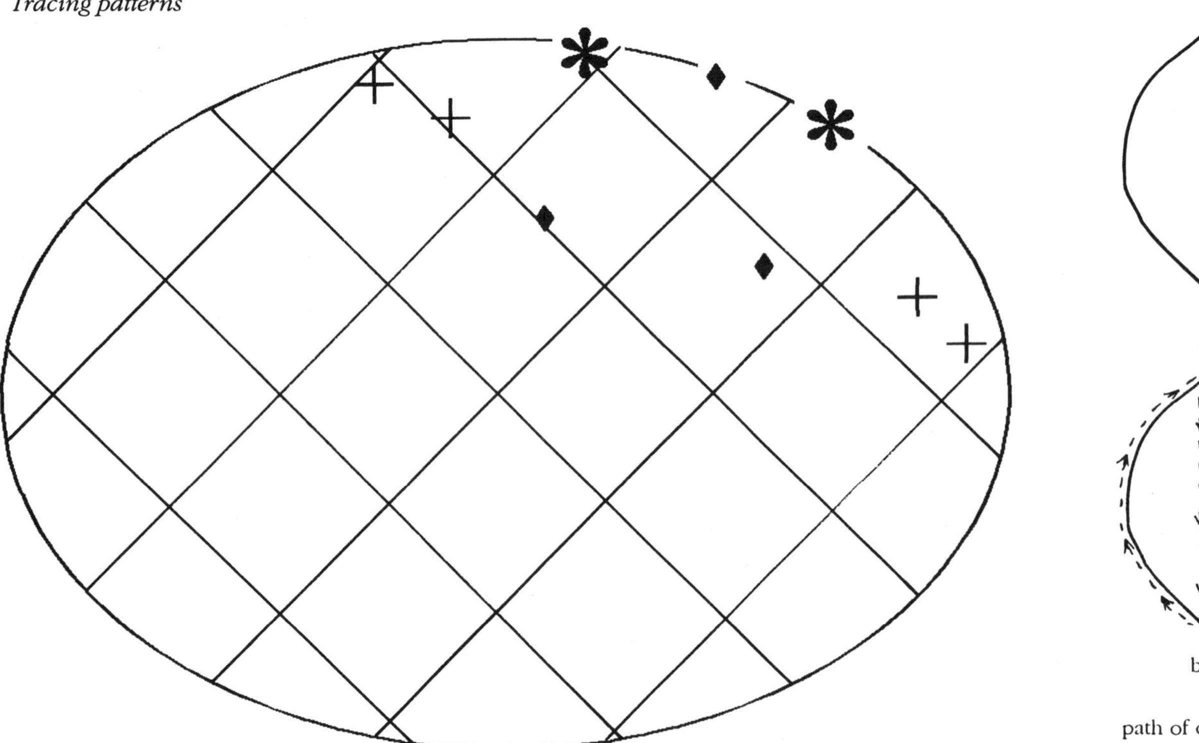

downwards like a stem. This will later be used to attach the leaf to the background embroidery.

9. Overcast the centre wire with close stitches, then outline the edge of the leaf in buttonhole stitch. Ensure that the bare wire and couching stitches have all been covered.

10. Repeat steps 8 and 9 with the other leaf shapes, then remove the calico from the embroidery frame and cut the completed leaves away from the background fabric. Using sharp pointed scissors, trim the leaves close to the outer edge of the buttonhole stitching.

11. Reposition the calico in the embroidery frame and make three more leaves in the same way.

12. Apply Fray Stoppa to one long edge of the strip of ivory silk taffeta in a band about 5 mm (3/16") deep. Allow to dry. Cut along the edge, through the Fray Stoppa, using pinking shears, curved nail scissors or decorative snips to give an uneven edge. Cut a piece 21.5 cm (8½") long from the strip and join the short ends together with a French seam. Gather the long raw edge and draw the fabric up into a circle. Stitch across the gathers in the centre to hold in place. Fasten the thread securely, and leave it hanging on the underside of the work.

13. Cut a piece of organdie ribbon 16.5 cm (6½") long. Join the short ends. Fold in half lengthways, with the raw edges enclosed, and gather along the long edge through both thicknesses. Pull up the gathers and flatten, leaving a small gap in the centre. Stitch to hold in place, then centre the organdie on top of the gathered silk strip and sew both pieces together at the centre. Finish thread securely, pass it to the back of the work and unthread the needle.

14. Make two more flowers in the same way, then fill their centres with about a dozen pearl beads, closely packed. Set flowers aside until the cushion is made up.

15. Ease the stem wires of the leaves through the background fabric and wadding at the crosses marked on the pattern. Place one leaf at each of the outer marks, and two at each of the inner ones. Pull the wires through so that the leaves rest on the cords and sew the wires down firmly on the back of the work, underneath the cord, for 2.5 cm (1"). Trim away the remaining ends of wire.

16. Remove the silk fabric and wadding from the working frame and press to remove creases. Place the second rectangle of silk on top, right sides together, then add the remaining rectangle of wadding. Pin through all layers, then stitch around three sides of the cushion, taking 2 cm (¾") seams. Take care not to catch the wired leaves in the stitching—they can be pushed out of the way and repositioned when the cushion is finished. Trim the seams and clip the corners before turning the work through to the right side.

17. Insert polyester filling into the brooch cushion, filling it very firmly. Turn in the raw edges on the fourth side for 2 cm (¾") and pin in place. Ladder stitch the edges together.

18. Sew the flowers onto the brooch cushion at the diamond shaped marks, using the working threads. Finish off all ends of cotton, then position the leaves to show around the flowers.

11 *Tapestry box-lid*

Illustrated on page 41

MATERIALS

45 cm x 30 cm (18" x 12") mono canvas, 14 holes per 2.5 cm (1")
Appletons Crewel Wools, 1 skein each:
- dull rose pink 146
- Jacobean green 296
- grey green 356
- sea green 401
- cornflower 461
- autumn yellow 472
- early English green (dark) 542
- early English green (light) 544
- peacock blue (light) 641
- peacock blue (dark) 642
- honeysuckle yellow 695
- bright china blue 742
- rose pink 754
- biscuit brown 765
- heraldic gold 841
- pastel shades cream 871, 4 skeins

wooden box with recessed lid, 13.5 cm x 28 cm (5¼" x 11 1/16")
wadding 13.5 cm x 28 cm (5½" x 11 1/16")

1. Finish the box by staining or painting it, then set aside while completing the embroidery for the lid.

2. Bind the raw edges of the canvas with masking tape and mount the piece in a rectangular working frame. Measure to find the centre of the canvas and mark lightly with a pencil.

3. Following the chart, on which each square represents one stitch, embroider the design in tent stitch using 2 strands of wool.

4. When the motif is complete, count out 10 threads on each of the long sides, 15 threads on the short sides, and mark the canvas at these points. Following the threads of the canvas, draw lines to intersect and form a rectangular outline around the embroidery.

5. Starting at the top right-hand corner with cream wool 871, fill in the entire background area with basketweave tent stitch.

Tapestry box-lid chart

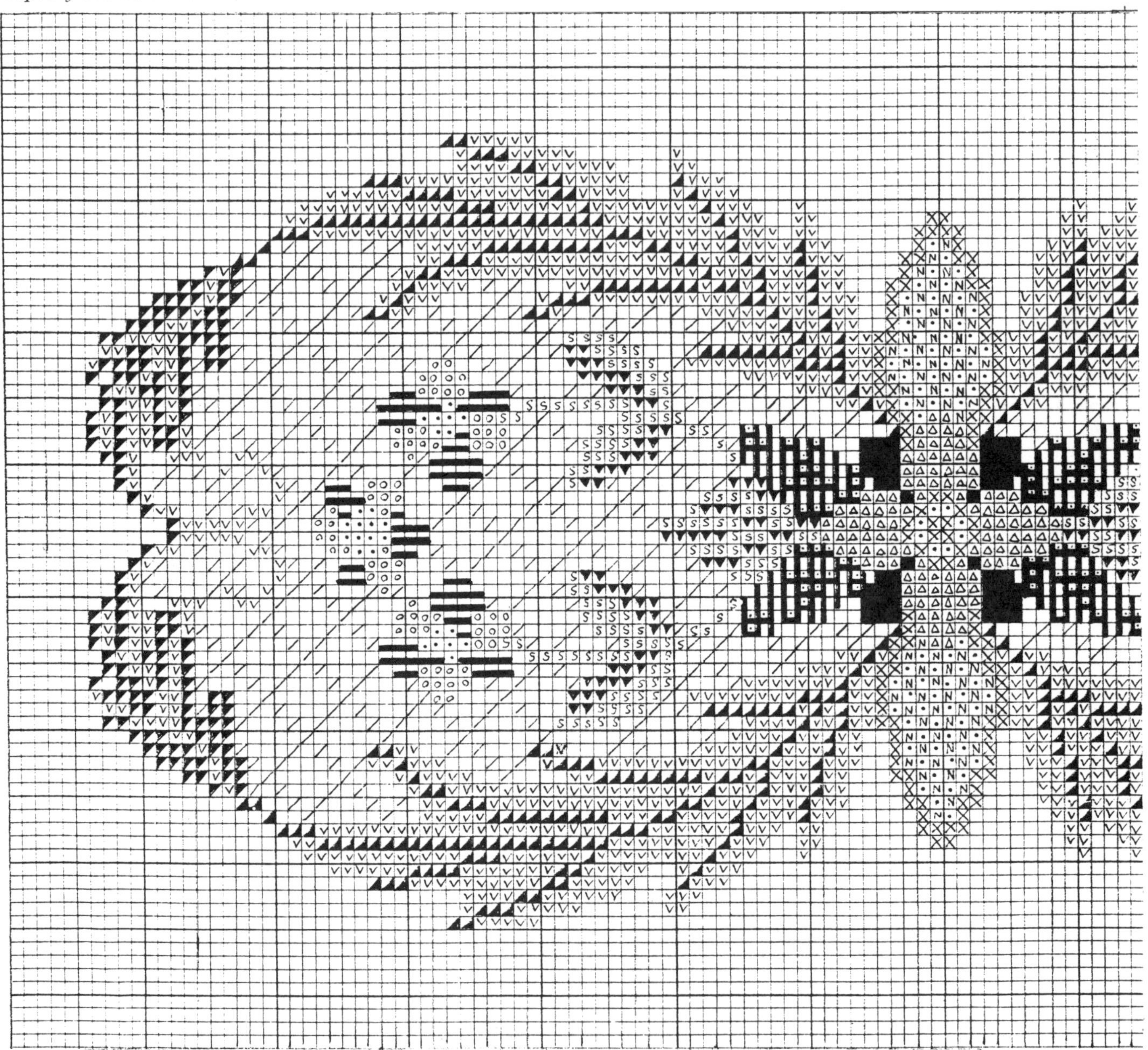

6. Remove the canvas from the frame. Block to shape if necessary, and trim the canvas to leave a border of 2 cm (¾") around the edge of the stitching.

7. Lightly glue the wadding to one side of the lid insert panel supplied with the box. Centre the embroidery over the padded side of the panel and lace the canvas in place using strong thread. Trim excess bulk from the corners to ensure that the panel will lie as flat as possible.

8. Glue the embroidery into the recessed box-lid and weight it under a pile of books until the glue is completely dry.

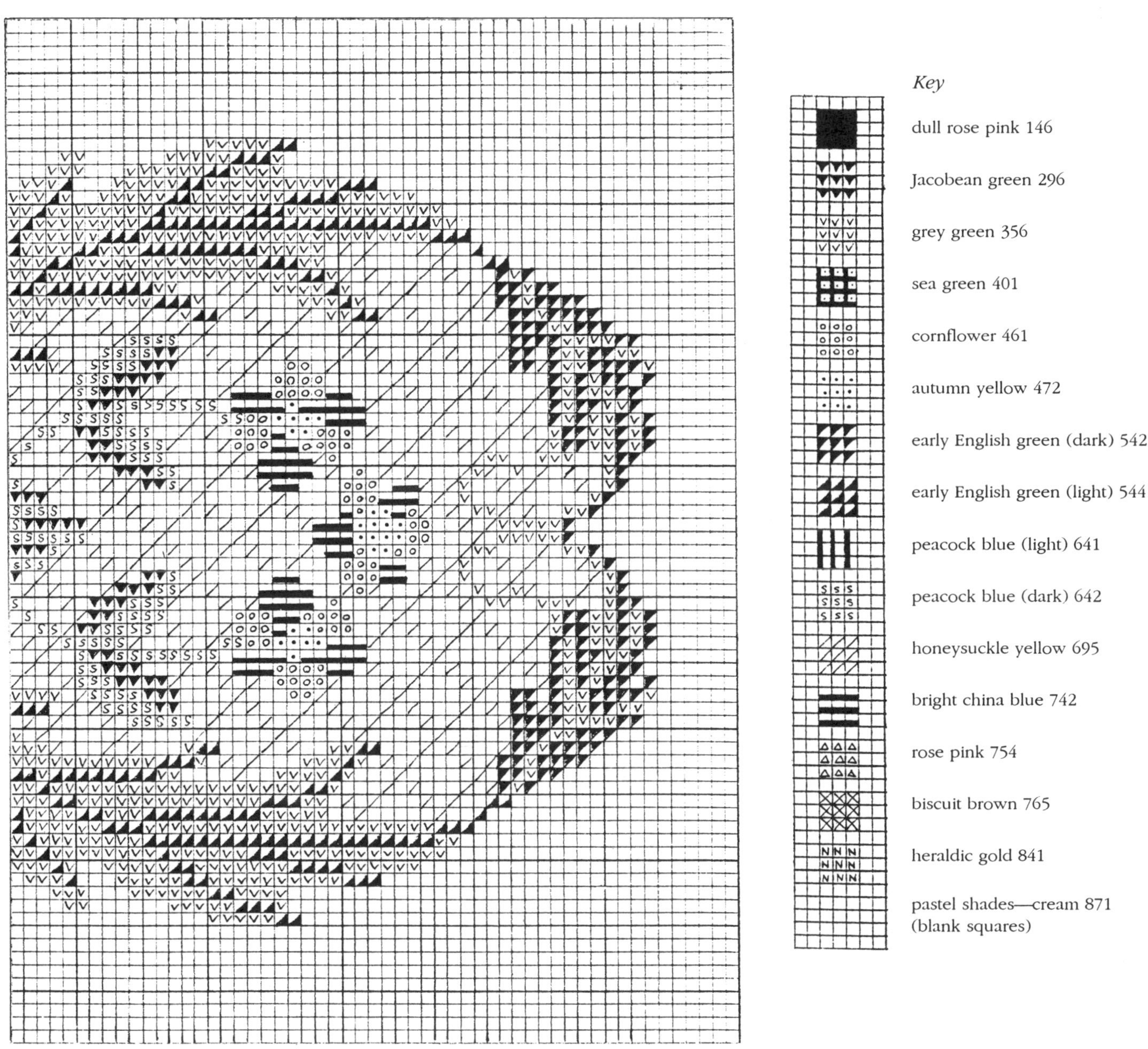

each square on the chart represents one stitch

12 *Crewel-work candlescreen*

Illustrated on page 42

Stitch and colour placement guide

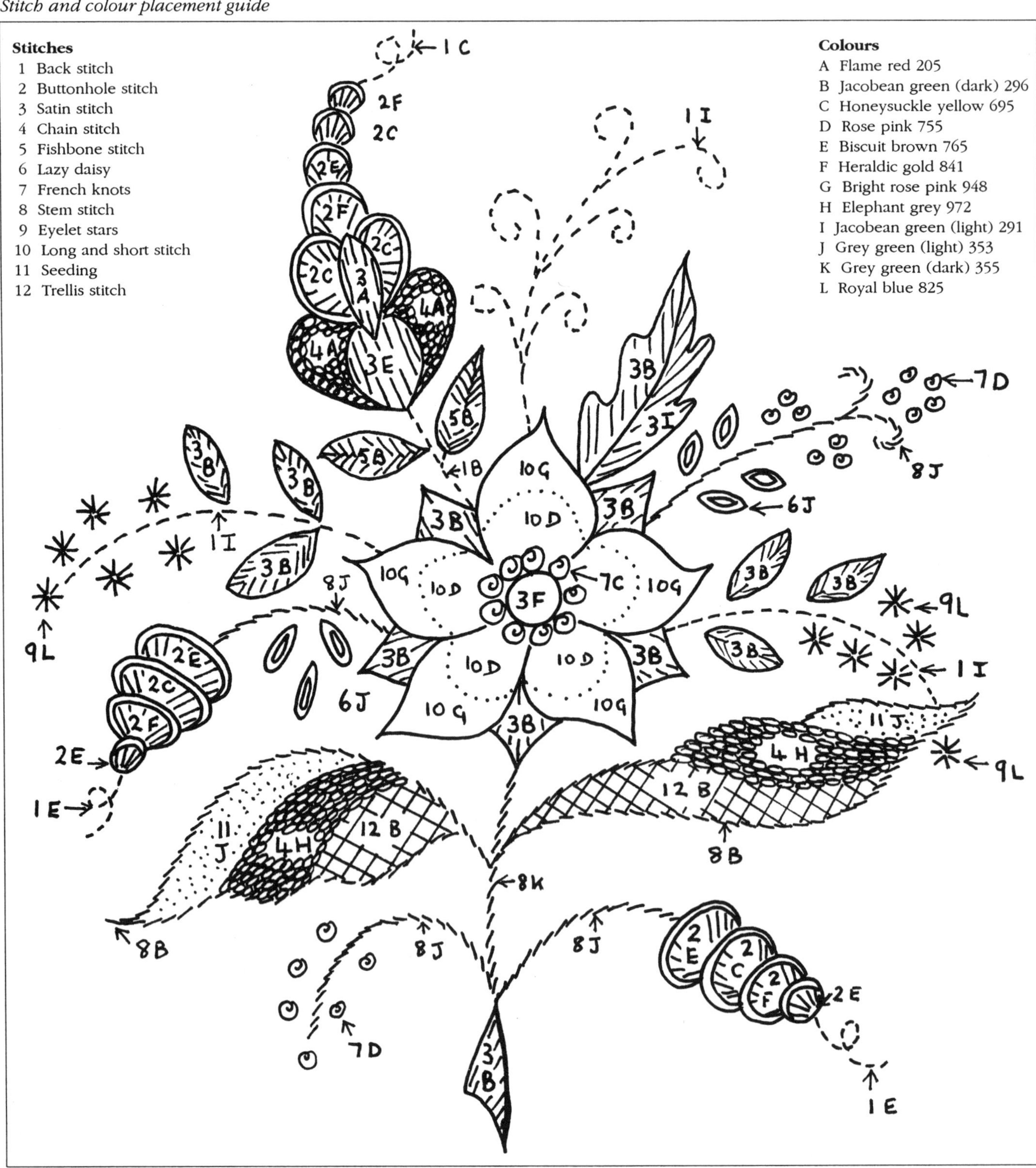

Shoe sweeteners (page 26) can be stuffed with lavender or a favourite potpourri

Chatelaine (page 32) embroidered in silk threads and trimmed with ribbon and matching tassels

Tapestry box-lid worked in wool in an unusual floral design (page 35)

Embroidered edging gives a pretty lift to a handtowel (page 44)

A pretty embroidered candlescreen (page 38) to deflect draughts

Detail of embroidery

MATERIALS

16 cm x 20 cm (6" x 8") beige linen-type fabric
Appletons Crewel Wool, 1 skein each:

flame red 205	rose pink 755
Jacobean green (light) 291	biscuit brown 765
Jacobean green(dark) 296	royal blue 825
grey green (light) 353	heraldic gold 841
grey green (dark) 355	bright rose pink 948
honeysuckle yellow 695	elephant grey 972

Sudberry House small wooden candlescreen

1. Trace the pattern and transfer it to the centre of the piece of fabric.
2. Following the stitch and colour placement guide, embroider the motif onto the fabric using one strand of wool throughout.
3. When the embroidery is complete, press lightly on the wrong side.
4. Mount the embroidery into the candlescreen following the manufacturer's instructions.

Tracing pattern

ACTUAL SIZE

13 Embroidered towel edging

Illustrated on page 41

MATERIALS

handtowel 45 cm x 65 cm (17¾" x 25½")
50 cm (20") x 5 cm (2") white Aida band, 14 stitches to 2.5 cm (1")
Anchor stranded cotton, 1 skein each:

pale pink 23	mid yellow 301
mid pink 26	dark yellow 302
dark pink 29	pale olive green 842
lime green 279	dark olive green 844
pale yellow 292	blue 939

1. Following the chart, work the design along the Aida band, starting with Section A, 2 cm (¾") in from the raw edge. Use 2 strands of thread throughout. Repeat the Section B motif 6 times. Finish by working Section C once.
2. Press the finished embroidery on the reverse side, then centre the band across the towel. Pin the lower edge to just cover the woven band in the towel itself. Turn in the ends of the embroidered band, trimming slightly if necessary.
3. Using matching sewing cotton, stitch the embroidered band in place on the towel and remove the pins.

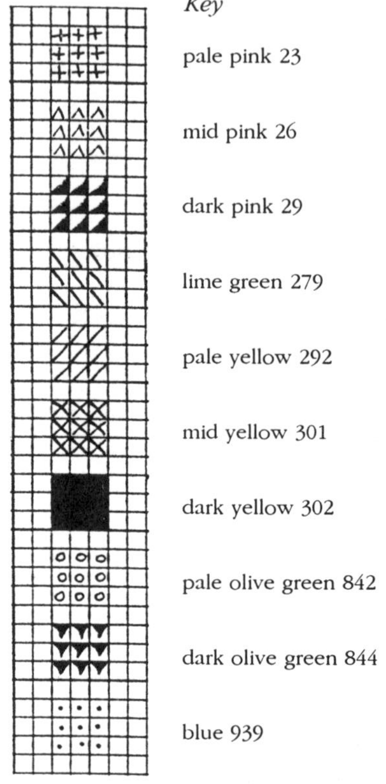

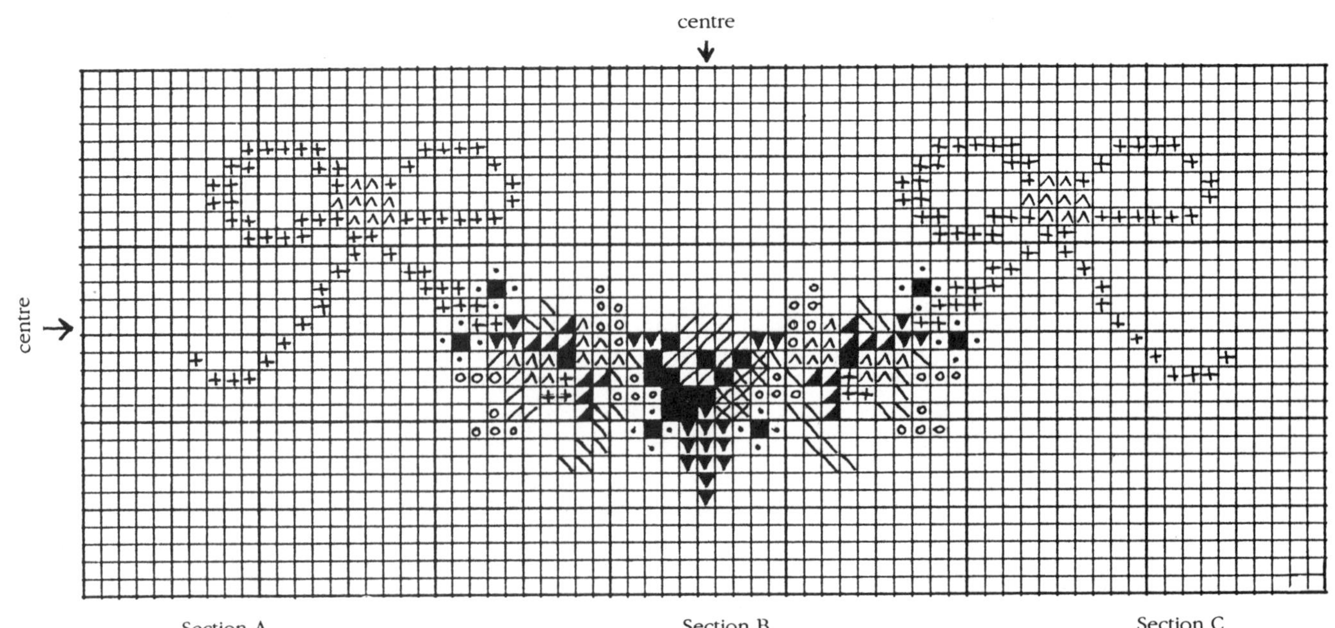

14 Oven cloth *Illustrated on page 52*

MATERIALS

30 cm x 40 cm (12" x 16") cream wool blanketing fabric
Appletons Crewel Wool, 1 skein each:

mid olive green 343	bright rose pink (light) 941
honeysuckle yellow 695	bright rose pink (dark) 944
royal blue 821	drab fawn 952
heraldic gold 841	

60 cm (24") blue and white gingham fabric 90 cm (36") wide
40 cm x 85 cm (16" x 33½") all-wool wadding
2 m (2¼ yds) blue gingham bias binding

1. Trace the pattern and transfer twice to woollen fabric.
2. Following the colour and stitch placement diagram, embroider the design using 2 strands of wool throughout.
3. When the embroidery is complete, press it lightly on the reverse side, then cut out the two sections.
4. Using the wool pieces as patterns, cut 2 pieces from the gingham fabric. Pin one piece of gingham to one of the embroidered woollen pieces, wrong sides facing, and sew across the short straight edge. Open out and pin the gingham to the back of the embroidered piece, enclosing the turnings. Top stitch close to the straight edge through all layers of the material. Tack the fabric pieces together around the curved edges. Repeat with the other embroidered section.
5. From the remaining gingham, cut two strips across the width of the fabric, 17.5 cm (6⁷/₈") deep. Cut two identical pieces from the wadding.
6. Place one piece of gingham face down on a level surface, and top it with both pieces of wadding and the second piece of gingham, face up. Pin and tack the layers together securely. Machine stitch lines 2.5 cm (1") apart along the length of the shape to quilt the layers together, using the gingham squares as a guide for stitching.
7. Place the quilted fabric on a level surface, and pin the embroidered sections to each end, with right sides facing upwards. Trim the quilted fabric to match the curves on the wool sections. Stitch through all thicknesses 7 mm (¼") from the edge.
8. Pin the bias binding along the edge, turning in the end neatly, then stitch in place through all layers. Turn the oven cloth over, folding the bias strip over the raw edges, and slip stitch in place. If desired, add a hanging loop made from a 15 cm (6") strip of bias binding, folded in half and slip-stitched along the long edge.

Tracing pattern

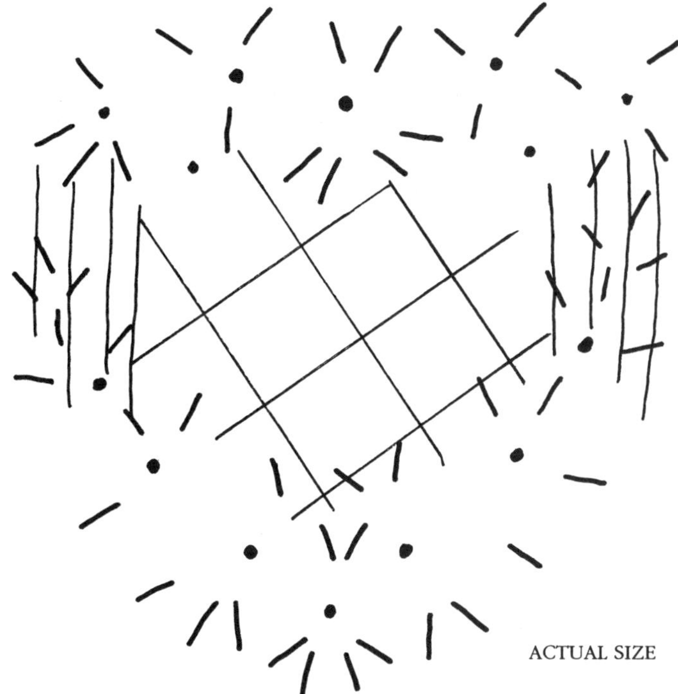

ACTUAL SIZE

Key
All flower petals are worked in lazy daisy stitch:
centre flowers top and bottom, bright rose pink (light) 941
bottom flowers, either side of centre, bright rose pink (dark) 944
small side flowers at top, heraldic gold 841
small side flowers at bottom, honeysuckle yellow 695
All large flower centres: French knots, honeysuckle yellow 695
Leaves: lazy daisy, mid olive green 343
Heart: stem stitch, drab fawn 952
Trellis: back stitch, drab fawn 952

15 *Tea cosy* *Illustrated on page 52*

MATERIALS

40 cm x 60 cm (16" x 24") cream wool blanketing
Appletons crewel wool, 1 skein each:
- red fawn 302
- mid olive green (light) 341
- mid olive green (medium) 343
- autumn yellow 471
- honeysuckle yellow 695
- royal blue 821
- heraldic gold 841
- pastel (cream) 871
- bright rose pink (light) 941
- bright rose pink (medium) 944
- bright rose pink (dark) 945
- drab fawn 952

70 cm (28") blue and white gingham 90 cm (36") wide
45 cm (18") wadding 115 cm (45") wide
80 cm x 10 cm (32" x 4") bonding web

1. Enlarge the pattern for the tea cosy on the next page then trace it onto a folded piece of paper. Cut out through both thicknesses, following the marked lines.
2. Open out the pattern and use it to cut two pieces from the woollen fabric. Mark the ends of the centre lines with pins at the edges.
3. Trace the design motifs for the tea cosy from pages 48–49 and transfer them to the woollen pieces, matching the centre lines of the motifs to the points pinned on the fabric. Remove the pins.
4. Following the stitch and colour placement guides, embroider the motifs. Use one strand of wool for all yellow flowers and flower centres, mid green feather-stitched foliage and blue French knots, and 2 strands for the remainder of the embroidery.
5. When the embroidery is complete, lightly press the pieces on the wrong side.
6. From the gingham, cut three strips 12 cm (4¾") deep across the width of the fabric, and set aside. Use the embroidered sections of the tea cosy as patterns to cut matching pieces from the remaining gingham and the wadding.
7. Place a piece of wadding on a flat surface and centre a gingham piece over it. Cover this with the front of the tea cosy, right side down, pin the three pieces together, and sew across the straight edges through all layers.
8. Repeat this procedure for the other side of the tea cosy. Turn the gingham sections over so that the wadding is enclosed in the middle of the layers. Tack the three layers of fabric together all around the curved edge, then top stitch through all layers close to the bottom fold to keep the seam allowances in place.
9. Trim the selvedges from two of the 12 cm (4¾") gingham strips and seam them together along one short edge. Sew a row of gathering stitches along each long edge of the strip, leaving a seam allowance of 1.5 cm (⅝").
10. Pull up the gathering stitches and pin one edge of the strip in place around the curved edge of one side of the tea cosy, with the right sides together, distributing the gathers evenly and leaving 1.5 cm (⅝") overhanging at each end. Sew in place, stitching through all layers of fabric. Repeat for the other side of the tea cosy, keeping the gathers even.
11. Press under a 1.5 cm (⅝") seam allowance on all four sides of the remaining gingham strip. Cut a strip of wadding 9 cm (3½") wide. Fuse this to the wrong side of the gingham strip with the bonding web. Turn the tea cosy to the wrong side, and pin the gingham strip in place so that it covers the raw edges of the gathered strip, with the wadding in between the two sections. Slip stitch the strip in place all around the edges.

Cutting pattern

NOT ACTUAL SIZE

Enlarge by photocopying at 133%
(grid enlargement: 3 cm = 4 cm; 1½" = 2")

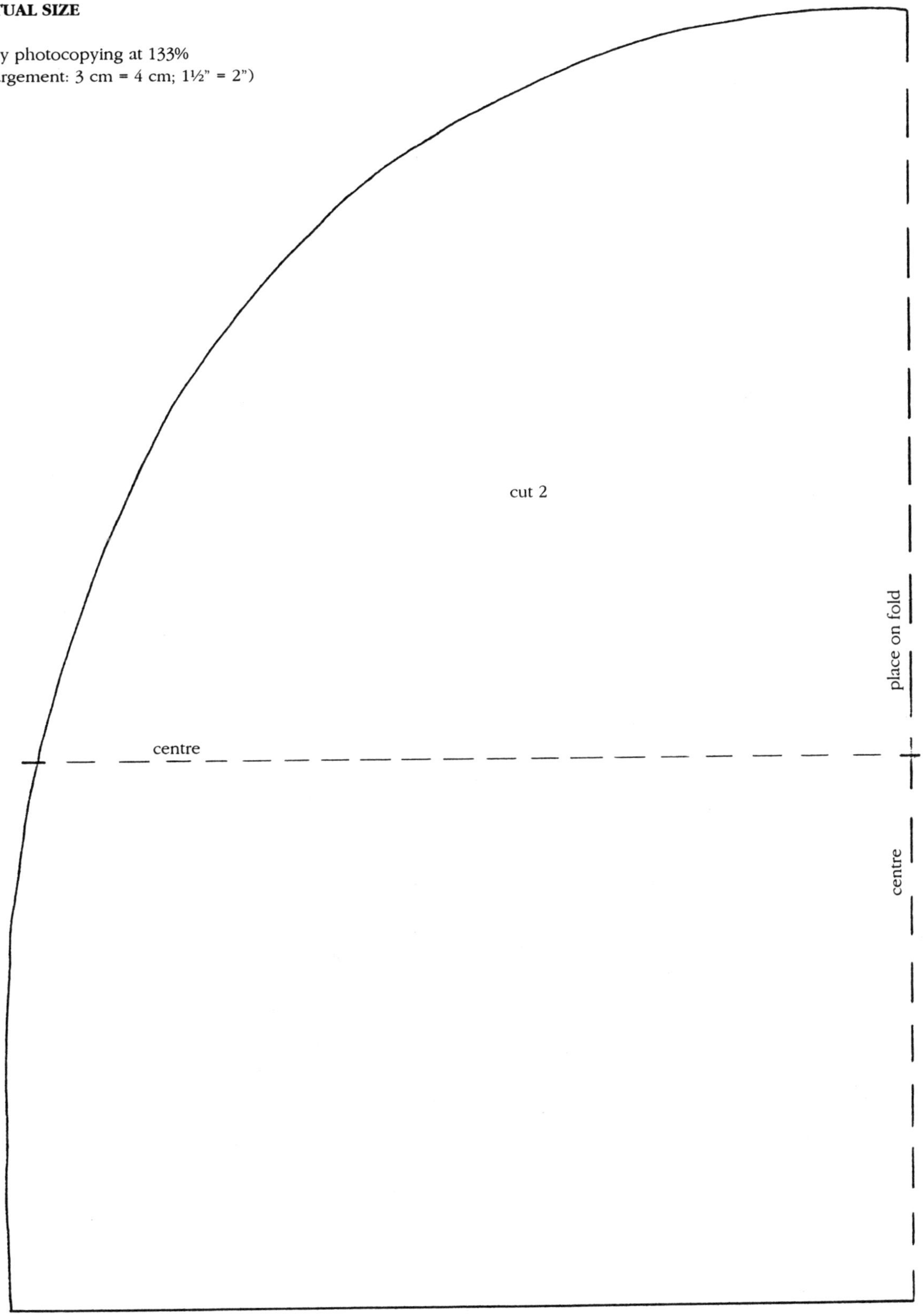

cut 2

centre

place on fold

centre

Embroidery tracing pattern for front of tea cosy

ACTUAL SIZE

Colour placement and stitch guide

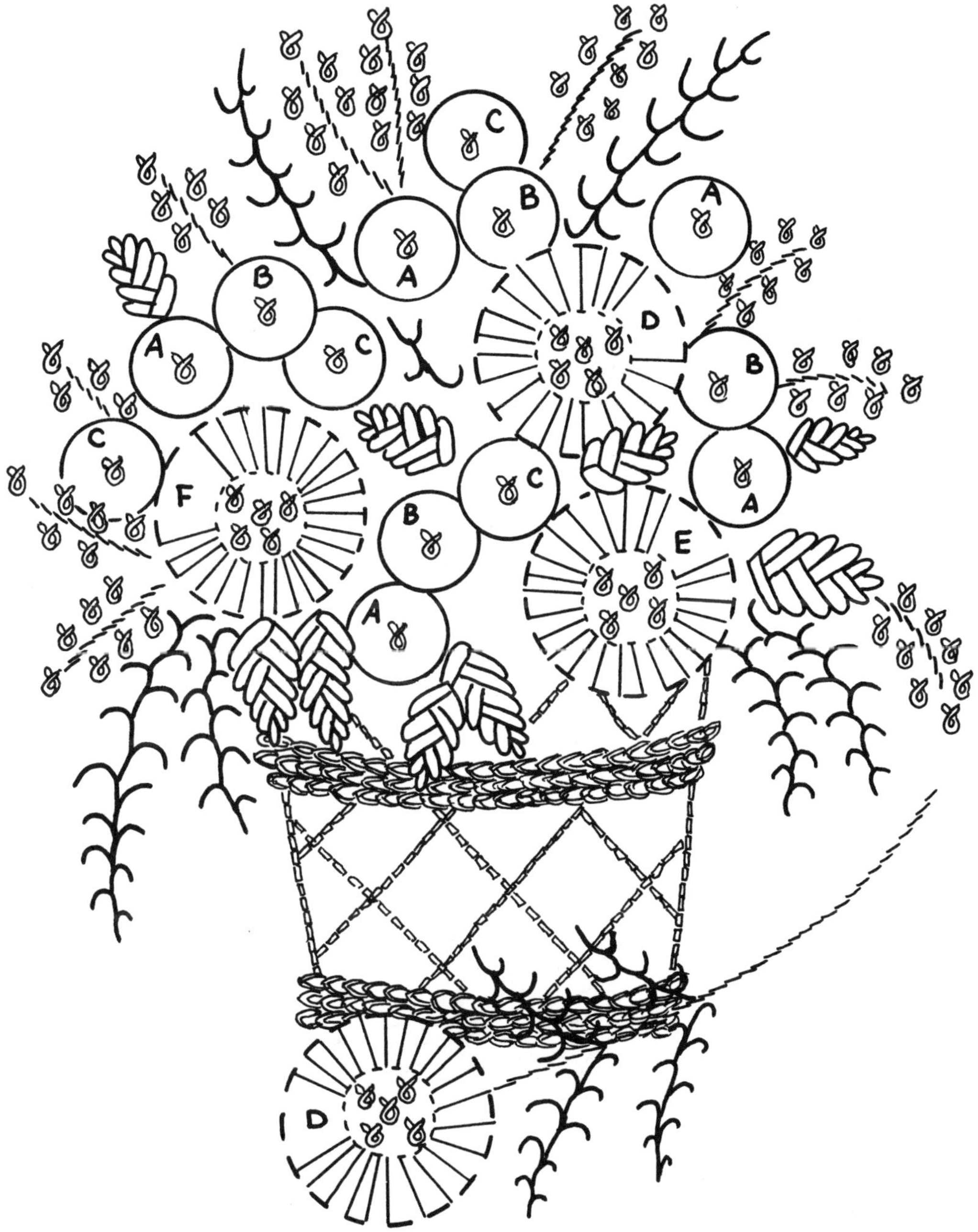

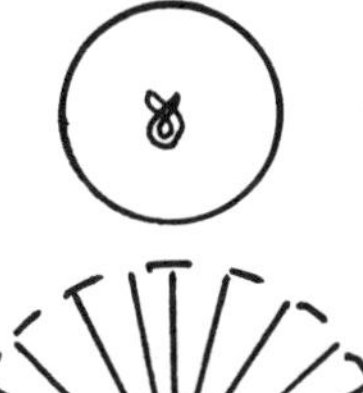

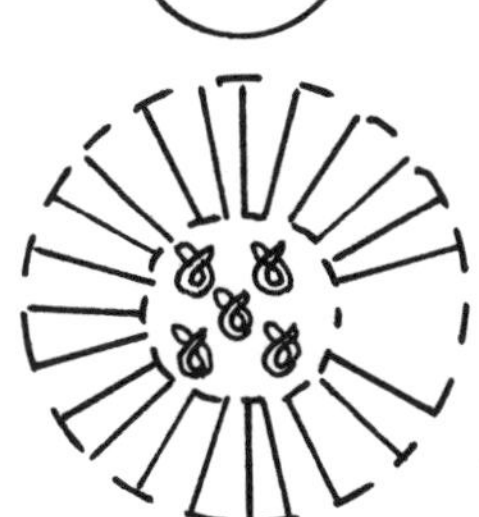

Chrysanthemums

A petals: lazy daisy, autumn yellow 471
centre: French knot, red fawn 302

B petals: lazy daisy, pastel cream 871
centre: French knot, autumn yellow 471

C petals: lazy daisy, heraldic gold 841
centre: French knot, autumn yellow 471

D petals: straight stitch, bright rose pink (dark) 945
centre: French knots, honeysuckle yellow 695

E petals: straight stitch, bright rose pink (mid) 944
centre: French knots, honeysuckle yellow 695

F petals: straight stitch, bright rose pink (pale) 941
centre: French knots, honeysuckle yellow 695

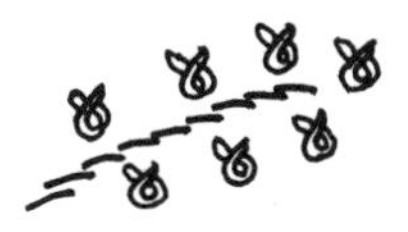

Delphinium spikes
stems: stem stitch, mid olive green 341
flowers: French knots, royal blue 821

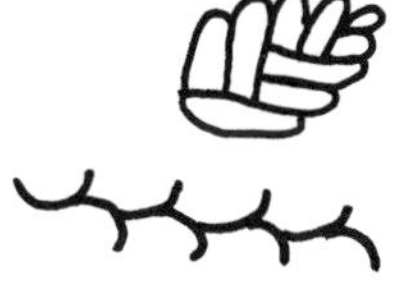

Leaves: fishbone stitch,
mid olive green (pale) 341

Fern fronds: featherstitch,
mid olive green (medium) 343

Basket top & bottom: chain stitch,
drab fawn 952

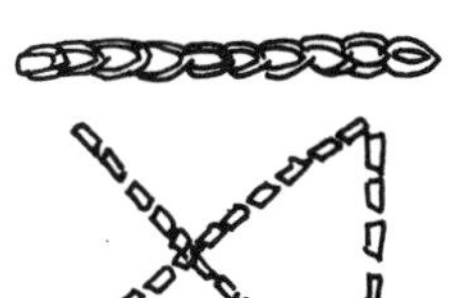

Basket sides: back stitch,
drab fawn 952

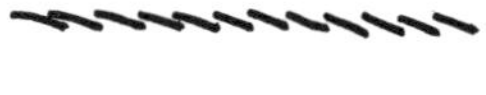

Lower flower stem: stem stitch,
mid olive green (medium) 343

Tracing pattern for back of tea cosy

ACTUAL SIZE

Colour placement and stitch guide

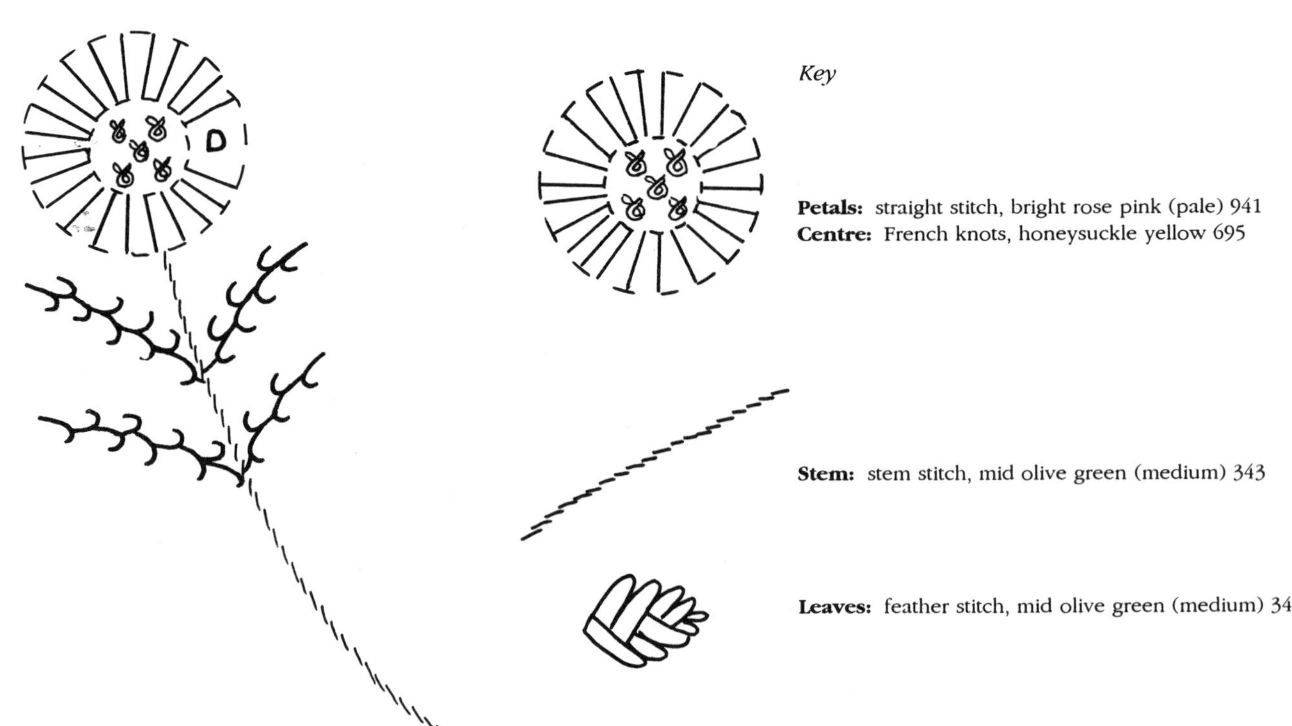

A heart-shaped garland of roses on a deep-frilled cushion (page 56)

The smocked panel shown here on a long cushion (page 62) may be worked to any width you need

Wool-embroidered tea cosy (page 46) features a single flower on the back

Double oven mitt in wool and gingham (page 45)

Matching motifs of the pansy traycloth (page 55) are embroidered in stranded cottons

Detail of pansy motif

The ribbon-weave panel of this notebook cover (page 69) is decorated with silk thread embroidery and a posy of roses

An oval insert embroidered in silk threads and ribbons is a feature of this writing box (page 68)

16 Pansy tray cloth

Illustrated on page 53

Pansy tray cloth chart

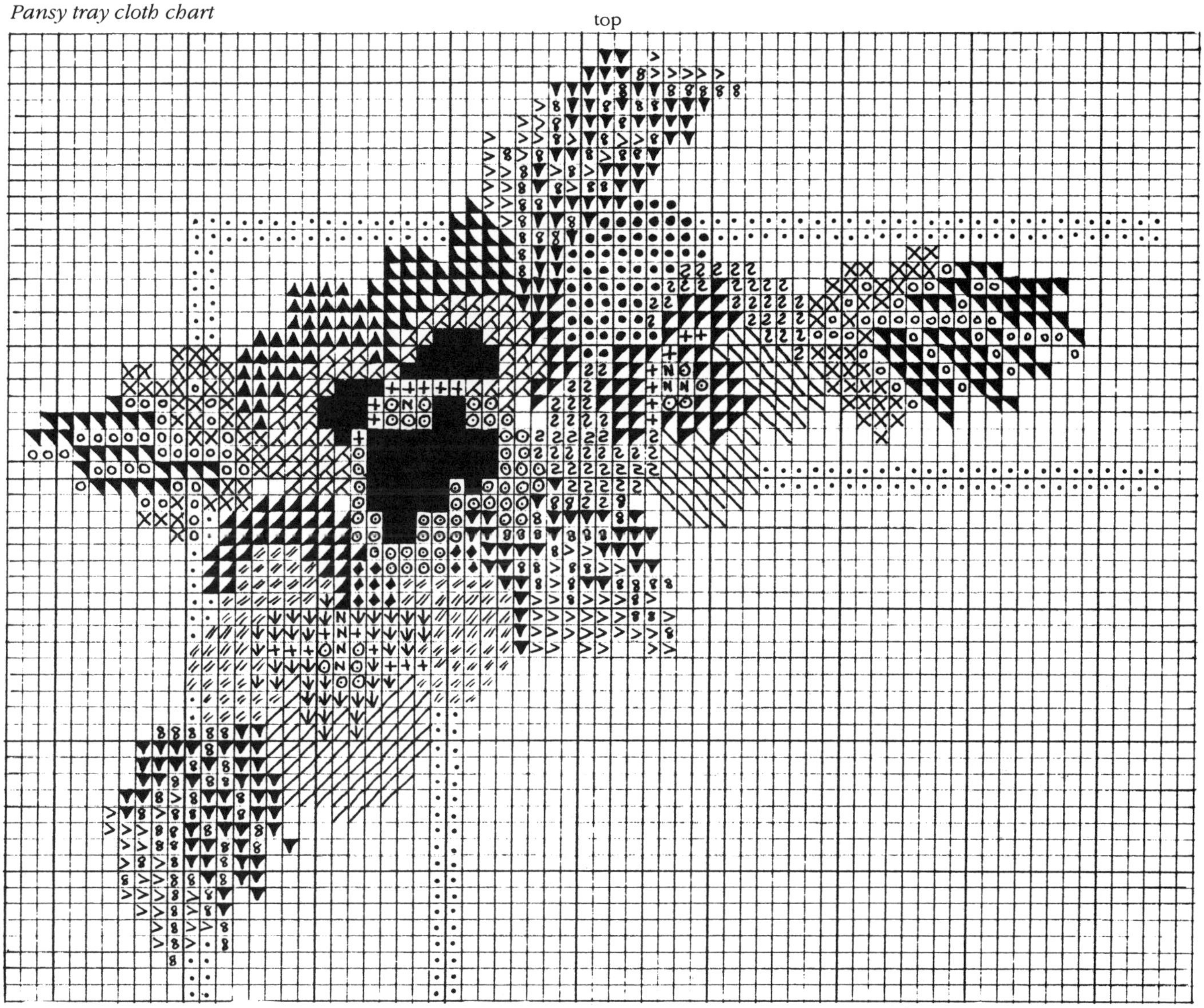

top

Key

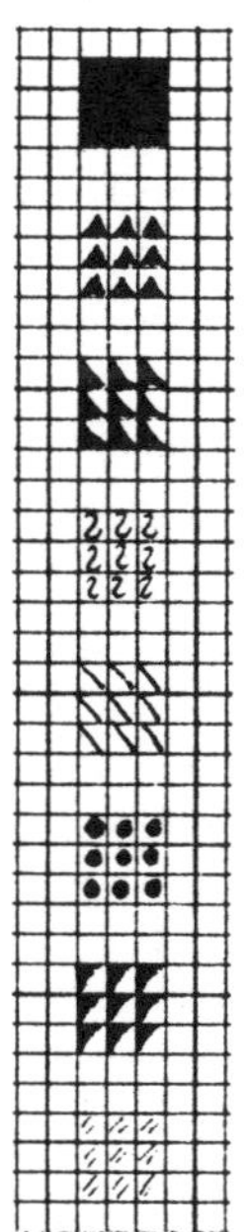

dark maroon 44

light pink 75

dark pink 76

light mauve 97

mid mauve 99

dark mauve 101

dark purple 102

mid purple 109

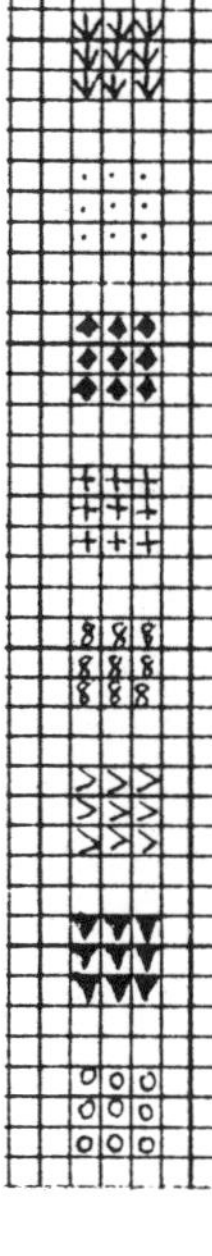

mid blue violet 112

sky blue 117

dark blue violet 119

grey 234

light lime green 254

mid lime green 255

emerald green 258

pale olive green 260

mid olive green 267

dark olive green 269

lemon yellow 293

bright yellow 298

light lilac 342

cream 386

dark lilac 1030

MATERIALS

42 cm x 29.5 cm (16¾" x 11½") white Aida cloth, 14 stitches per 2.5 cm (1")

Anchor Stranded Cotton, 1 skein each:

dark maroon 44	light lime green 254
light pink 75	mid lime green 255
dark pink 76	emerald green 258
light mauve 97	pale olive green 260
mid mauve 99	mid olive green 267
dark mauve 101	dark olive green 269
dark purple 102	lemon yellow 293
mid purple 109	bright yellow 298
mid blue violet 112	light lilac 342
sky blue117	cream 386
dark blue violet 119	dark lilac 1030
grey 234	

1. Establish the corners of the design by counting in 30 threads from each side of the fabric.
2. Following the chart, and using 2 strands of thread throughout, embroider the motif starting at the top left-hand corner of the tray cloth.
3. Turn the work and embroider the motif a second time in the corner diagonally opposite the first.
4. Continue the bands of cross-stitch in sky blue 117 from each motif to meet at the remaining corners to complete the embroidery.
5. Count out 14 threads from the outer edge of each band of sky blue cross-stitch and fold the hem allowance to the wrong side. Turn under a narrow hem on the raw edges and press.
6. Mitre the corners, then slip stitch the hem in place on the back of the work, using matching sewing cotton.

17 *Heart of roses cushion*

Illustrated on page 51

MATERIALS

1 m (40") self-patterned curtain fabric 115 cm (45") wide
Appletons Crewel Wool, 1 skein each:
- Jacobean green 296
- grey green 356
- cornflower 461
- light Early English green 542
- mid Early English green 544
- peacock blue 641
- royal blue 821

DMC Pearl Cotton No. 5, 1 skein each:
- white
- variegated pinks 062

Rajmahal Art Silk, 1 skein each:
- mango cream 141
- persimmon 144

Rajmahal Metal Hand Sewing thread, 1 reel gold
35 cm (14") zip fastener to match fabric
2 m (2¼ yds) white cotton lace 7.5 cm (3") wide
No. 16 cushion insert

1. Cut a piece of curtain fabric 40 cm (16") square. Trace the design and transfer it to the centre of the fabric.
2. Following the stitch and colour guides, embroider the design. It is advisable to use a hoop to maintain an even tension across the stitchery.
3. Lightly press the finished embroidery on the wrong side, laying it face down over a soft towel to help maintain the raised appearance of the stitches.
4. From the remaining fabric cut two pieces 22.5 cm x 40 cm (9" x 16"). With right sides facing, seam the sections together for 2.5 cm (1") from each of the short edges on one long side and insert the zip into the opening following the manufacturer's instructions.
5. Make a frill by cutting two 22 cm (8⅝") wide strips of fabric across the width of the material and joining them together along their short sides to form a loop. Fold in half lengthways, enclosing the seams.
6. Cut the lace to the same length as the fabric band plus a seam allowance of 2.5 cm (1"). Seam the short ends together neatly. Place the band of lace inside the band of fabric, matching the lower edge of the lace to the raw edge of the fabric, and with the wrong side of the lace facing the right side of the fabric. Mark eight points evenly spaced around the long edge of the band, then gather the edge, stitching through both lace and fabric.
7. Pin the gathered edge of the band around the completed cushion top with right sides together. Match the marked points to the corners and the mid-point of each side of the cushion. Pull up the gathers and tack through all layers. Check that the gathers are evenly distributed, and that the corners have enough fullness to curve properly when opened out.

8. With right sides facing, pin the back section of the cushion over the front, enclosing the frill. Open the zip part-way so that the completed cushion can be turned through, and tack through all layers. Turn to the right side and check that the frill is not caught up anywhere before making the final line of machine stitching around the edges of the cushion.

9. Neaten all raw edges. Turn to the right side and ease the cushion insert into position.

Stitch and colour placement guide
(Use 2 strands of thread for wool, silk and gold; use 1 strand only of pearl cotton.)

Roses
leaves: satin stitch, Appletons Jacobean green 296, grey green 356, light early English green 542, mid early English green 544
stems: back stitch, Appletons Jacobean green 296, mid early English green 544
petals: buttonhole stitch, DMC Pearl, variegated pinks 062
centres: satin stitch, DMC Pearl, variegated pinks 062

Daisies
leaves: fly stitch, Appletons peacock blue 641
petals: lazy daisy, DMC Pearl white
centres: French knots, Rajmahal mango cream 141

Forget-me-nots
petals: French knots, Appletons royal blue 821
centres: French knots, Rajmahal persimmon 144

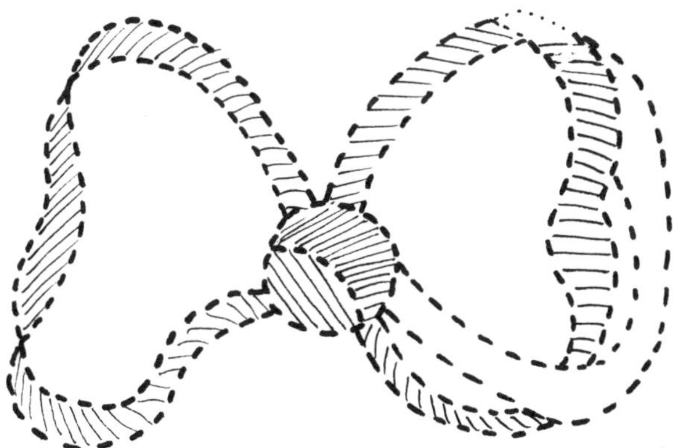

Bow
ribbons: satin stitch, Appletons cornflower 461
outline: back stitch, Rajmahal gold

Tracing pattern

ACTUAL SIZE

join

18 *Flower trellis cushion* *Illustrated on page 27*

MATERIALS

30 cm (12") square interlock canvas, 12 holes per 2.5 cm (1")
I reel Twilley's Gold-Dust Metallic Thread in silver
1 m (40") each of 3 mm ($^{3}/_{32}$") silk ribbons in:
dusty pink salmon pink bright pink
3 m (3¼ yds) each of 3 mm ($^{3}/_{32}$") silk ribbons in:
dark green medium green light green
Appletons Crewel Wool, 2 skeins pastel cream 871
1 m (40") pale blue velvet ribbon 13 mm (½") wide
1 m (40") matching linen-look fabric 115 cm (45") wide

Key

Motif A
Stems and leaves, medium green
Flowers, bright pink

Motif B
Stems and leaves, light green
Flowers, dusty pink

Motif C
Stems and leaves, dark green
Flowers, salmon pink

Motif D
Stems and leaves, light green
Flowers, dusty pink

Motif E
Stems and leaves, medium green
Flowers, bright pink

All border lines
Silver metallic thread

Background of all flower motifs and triangles
Appletons Crewel Wool, pastel cream 871

Needlepoint chart/guide
(each line of the graph represents one thread of the canvas)

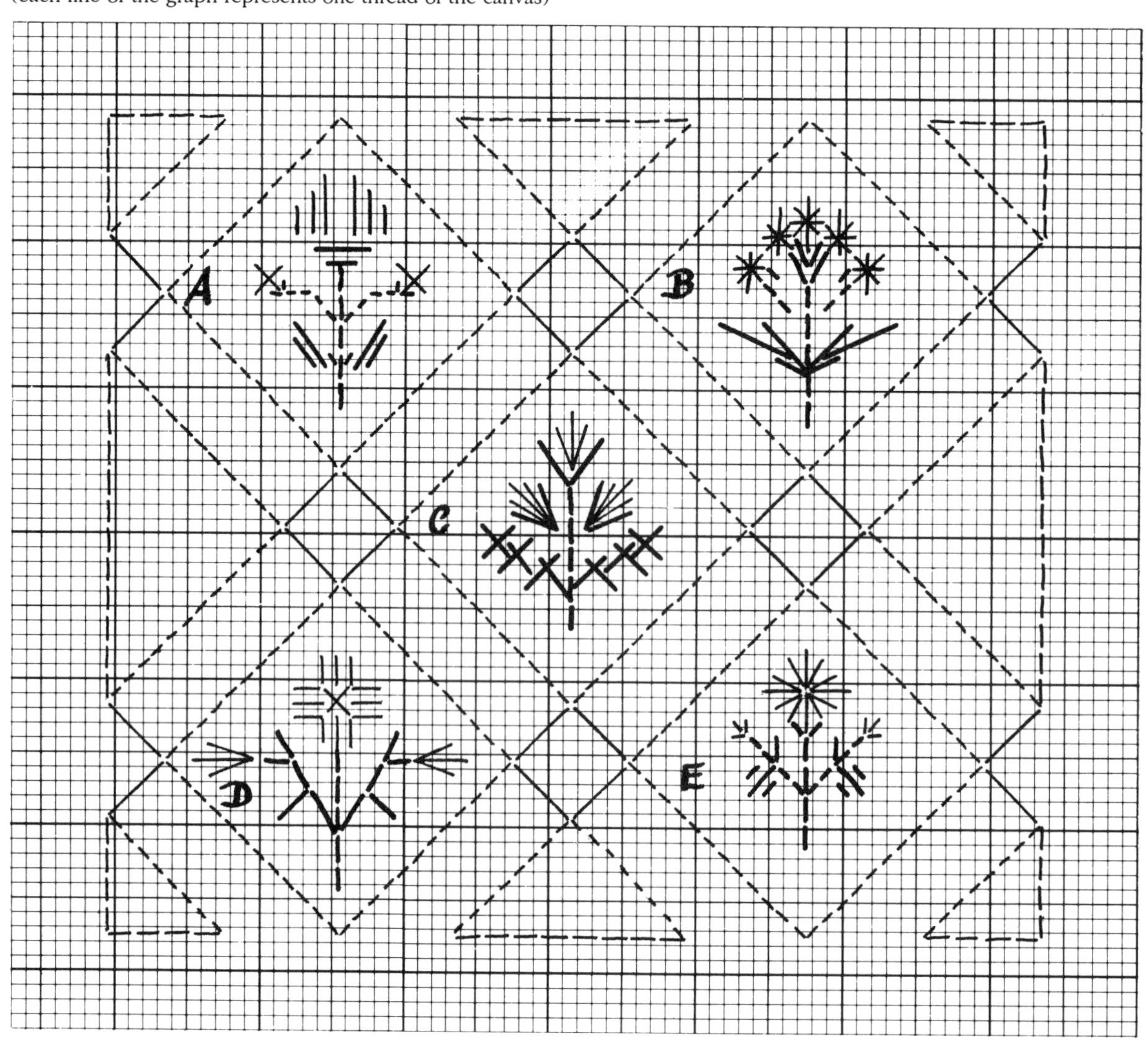

1. Mount canvas in a frame before starting to work this piece. Following the chart, on which each line represents one thread of the canvas, embroider the silk ribbon flower motifs in the colours shown.
2. Using silver thread, work diagonal lines of back stitch across the design, taking a single long stitch across each gap between diamonds as shown on the chart. Fill in the diamond shapes around each flower spray with tent stitch using 2 strands of crewel wool.
3. Cut the velvet ribbon to fit along the remaining spaces of the design, with an overlap of 1 cm (3/8") at each end. Place all ribbons in one direction, threading them under the long stitches in silver thread at each intersection, then overlay the ribbons in the opposite direction in the same way. Slip stitch the ends onto the canvas.
4. Starting at one corner, pin the remaining velvet ribbon around the edge of the rectangle, mitring each corner in turn, and covering the ends of the diagonal ribbons. Slip stitch the inner edges of the ribbon to the canvas using matching sewing cotton.
5. Carefully trim the canvas so that the raw edge is just inside the outer edge of the ribbon.
6. Cut a 35 cm (14") square of blue fabric and centre the canvas panel on it. Pin in position, then slip stitch in place through the outer edges of the velvet ribbon using matching sewing cotton.
7. Make a frill by cutting two 15 cm (5 7/8") wide strips of fabric across the width of the material, and joining them together along their short sides to form a loop. Fold in half lengthways, enclosing the seams.
8. Pin the frill around the edges of the cushion top, placing the seams at the centres of two opposite sides, and the marked points at the corners and the centres of the two remaining sides. Pull up the gathers evenly and tack in place through all thicknesses of material.
9. Cut two pieces of fabric 38 cm x 50 cm (15" x 20") for the back panels and fold each in half to measure 38 cm x 25 cm (15" x 9 7/8"). Pin the longer edges to the cushion front, covering the frill. Pin the shorter sides in place, overlapping the panels in the centre. Tack everything in place, then turn through to the right side and check that the frill is evenly distributed around the edge of the cushion and that there are no tucks or puckers. Turn back to the wrong side and sew through all layers around the previously tacked seam lines.
10. Neaten edges and clip corners. Remove tacking threads and turn to the right side. Insert cushion pad.

Note: The overlapped panels at the back can be fastened together with Velcro, press fasteners, buttons or ribbon ties. Buttonholes or ribbons should be sewn in place after folding the fabric in half at the beginning of step 9.

Bonus design

19 *Smocked cushion* *Illustrated on page 51*

MATERIALS

15 cm (6") white homespun cotton 115 cm (45") wide
DMC Stranded Cotton, 1 skein each:

dark pink 223	light green 471
light pink 224	dark blue 799
dark green 469	light blue 800

1 m (40") white gathered broderie anglaise edging 25 mm (1") wide
1 m (40") white broderie anglaise insertion 17 mm (5/8") wide
1 m (40") blue satin ribbon 7 mm (¼") wide
30 cm (12") blue linen-type fabric 115 cm (45") wide
matching sewing cotton
polyester filling

Smocking chart

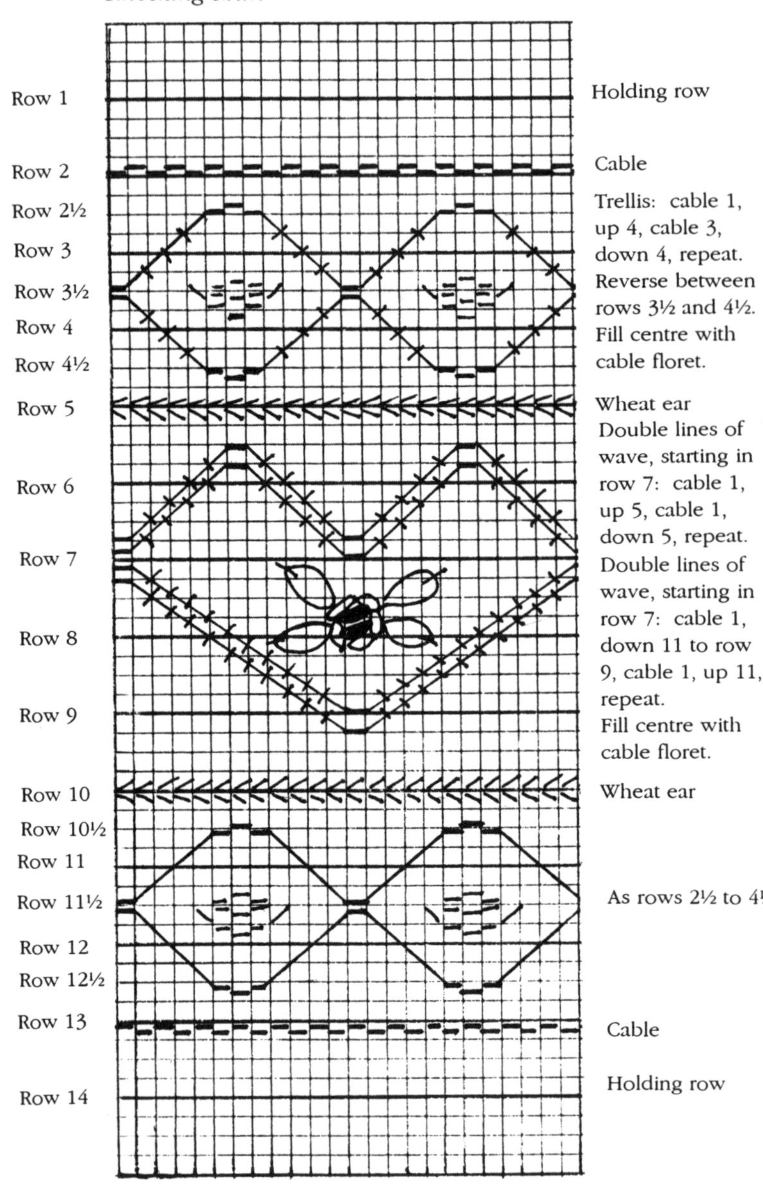

1. Pleat 14 rows across the full width of the white fabric.
2. Following the chart, smock the design onto the pleated fabric using the stitches and colours shown.
3. Withdraw smocking threads 2 to 13, leaving the top and bottom holding threads in place. Draw out the smocked fabric to a width of 30 cm (12") and steam press.
4. Thread the blue ribbon through the holes in the broderie anglaise insertion lace and pin it around the smocked panel starting at the bottom right hand corner and mitring each corner in turn. Fold under the raw edges and trim to form a neat mitred join at the starting point. Hand stitch the lace in place and remove pins.
5. Pin and stitch the gathered lace to the outer edge of the insertion lace in the same way.
6. Cut two panels 30 cm x 45 cm (12" x 18") from the blue fabric. Centre the smocked panel face upwards on the right side of one rectangle and pin in place. Stitch through the outer edge of the lace insertion by hand or machine to secure the smocked panel in position.
7. Place the second rectangle of blue fabric over the first, with the right sides facing inwards. Taking 1.5 cm (5/8") seams, join the two pieces together around three sides, leaving one short edge open. Clip the corners and turn to the right side.
8. Turn in and press the seam allowances on the remaining short side. Fill the cushion with polyester fibrefill. (This could be contained in a separate bag of calico made to the same dimensions as the outer covering if desired.) Ladder stitch the open edges together using matching sewing cotton.

Miniature garden scenes in a three-part frame (page 71) are embroidered in silk amd cotton and metallic threads

Detail of one of the embroidered panels

Roses and lavender in silk threads and ribbons on a perforated paper photo frame mat (opposite)

20 *Photo frame mat*

Illustrated on opposite page

MATERIALS

white perforated paper, 1 sheet 35 cm x 22.5 cm (13¾" x 9")
Anchor Stranded Cotton, 2 skeins:
white 01
Rajmahal art silks, 1 skein each:
laurel green 65
sugar melon 251
sassafras 805
3 mm (1/8") silk ribbon, 5 m (5½ yds) each:

light pink	dark yellow
dark pink	green
light yellow	mauve

photograph for framing
pale green mat board 29 cm x 32.5 cm (11½" x 12¾")
picture frame

1. Use 2 strands of white cotton to embroider the cross-stitch outer frame, following the graph on which each line represents one grid of the perforated paper. The chart shows just over half of the design; reverse it to work the remaining section. Stitch the outer scalloped border. (The four corner motifs must be completed before counting inwards from the centre of each side to establish the position of the rectangular cut-out.)

2. In 2 strands white cotton, work the rectangle in cross-stitch, then back stitch all the trellis lines. Embroider all the lines in one direction before turning the work and stitching in the opposite direction. Work the straight stitch groups in the scallops of the outer edges.

3. Change to one thread of Rajmahal sugar melon 251 and work the five groups of foundation stitches for the ribbon roses in each corner of the design. These are shown in the top corner of the chart.

4. Work the ribbon embroidered flowers following the stitch guides. Use short lengths of ribbon to avoid carrying lengths of ribbon across the back of the work. Start with the roses, using the foundation stitches already worked. Establish the outer points of the flower spray by stitching the lavender at each end, then fill in the rest of the flowers and leaves between these points. Working on each of the four motifs in turn will help to keep them looking the same. Extra flowers, buds or leaves can be added if necessary to fill in any gaps.

5. After completing the embroidery carefully cut away the inner rectangle using a sharp craft knife. Leave one grid line intact next to the stitching.

6. Trim the outer edge of the design in the same way, using sharp scissors.

7. Mount the photograph centrally on the rectangle of mat board, using double sided sticky tape in each corner. Apply small pieces of tape to the back of the embroidery behind the corner motifs and the centres of the long sides, then carefully position the panel over the photograph and press firmly in place. The assembled piece is then ready for framing.

Stitch placement and colour guide

Lavender

flowers: straight stitch, mauve ribbon

stems: feather stitch, sassafras 805

Spider's web roses

foundation stitches: sugar melon 251

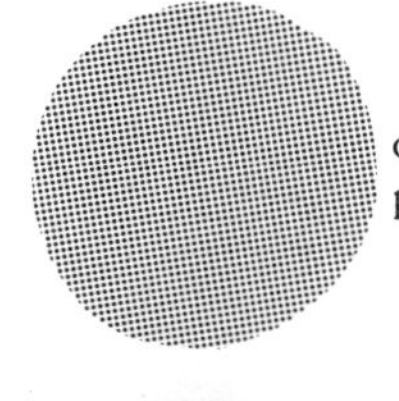

outer and middle flowers: pale pink ribbon

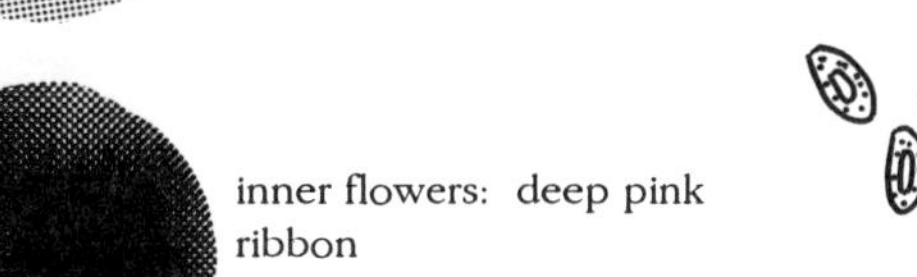

inner flowers: deep pink ribbon

Leaves

lazy daisy, laurel green 065

lazy daisy, green ribbon

Yellow petals

lazy daisy, dark yellow ribbon

lazy daisy, light yellow ribbon

Stitch chart

(each line on the graph represents one grid of the perforated paper)

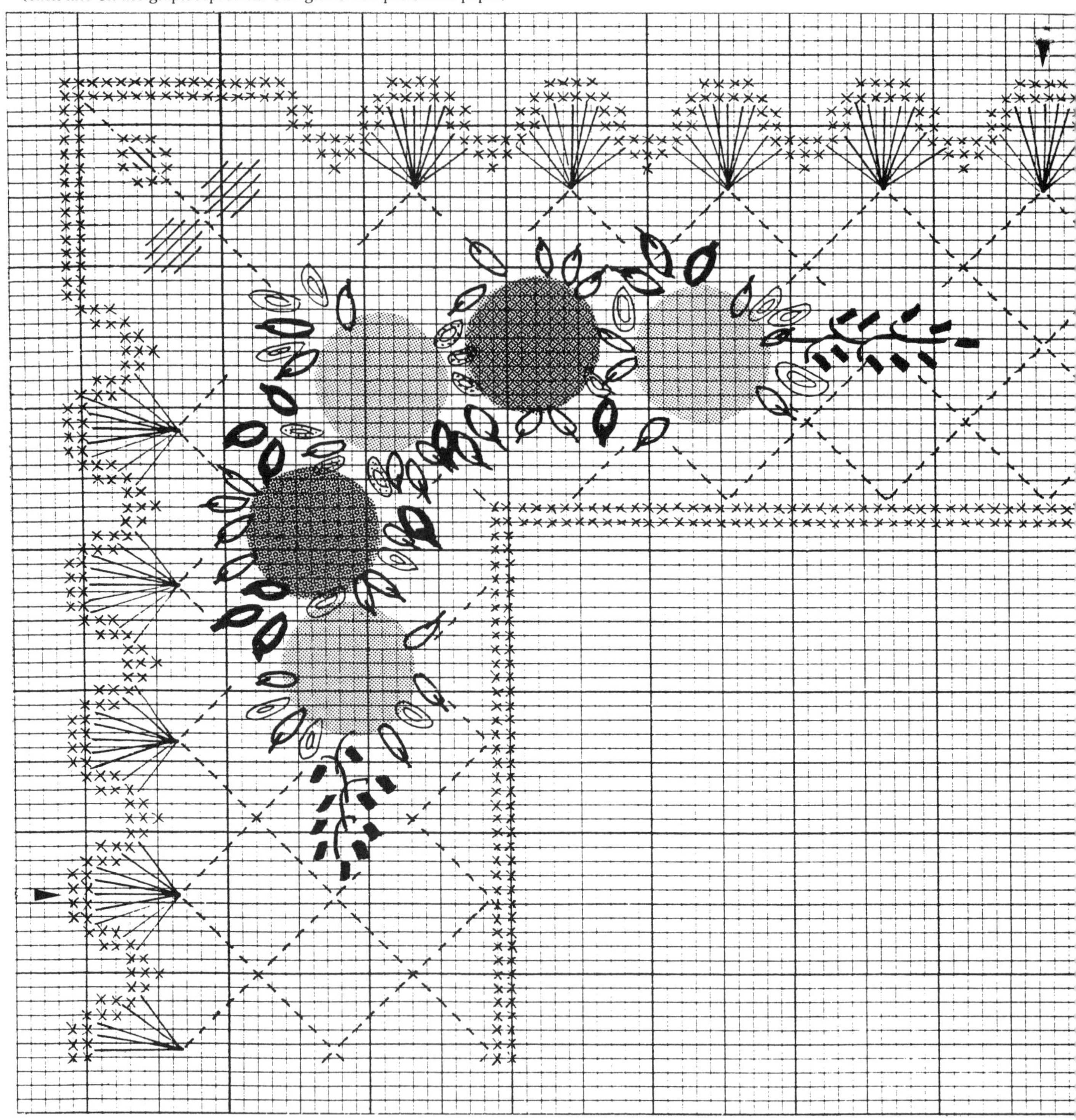

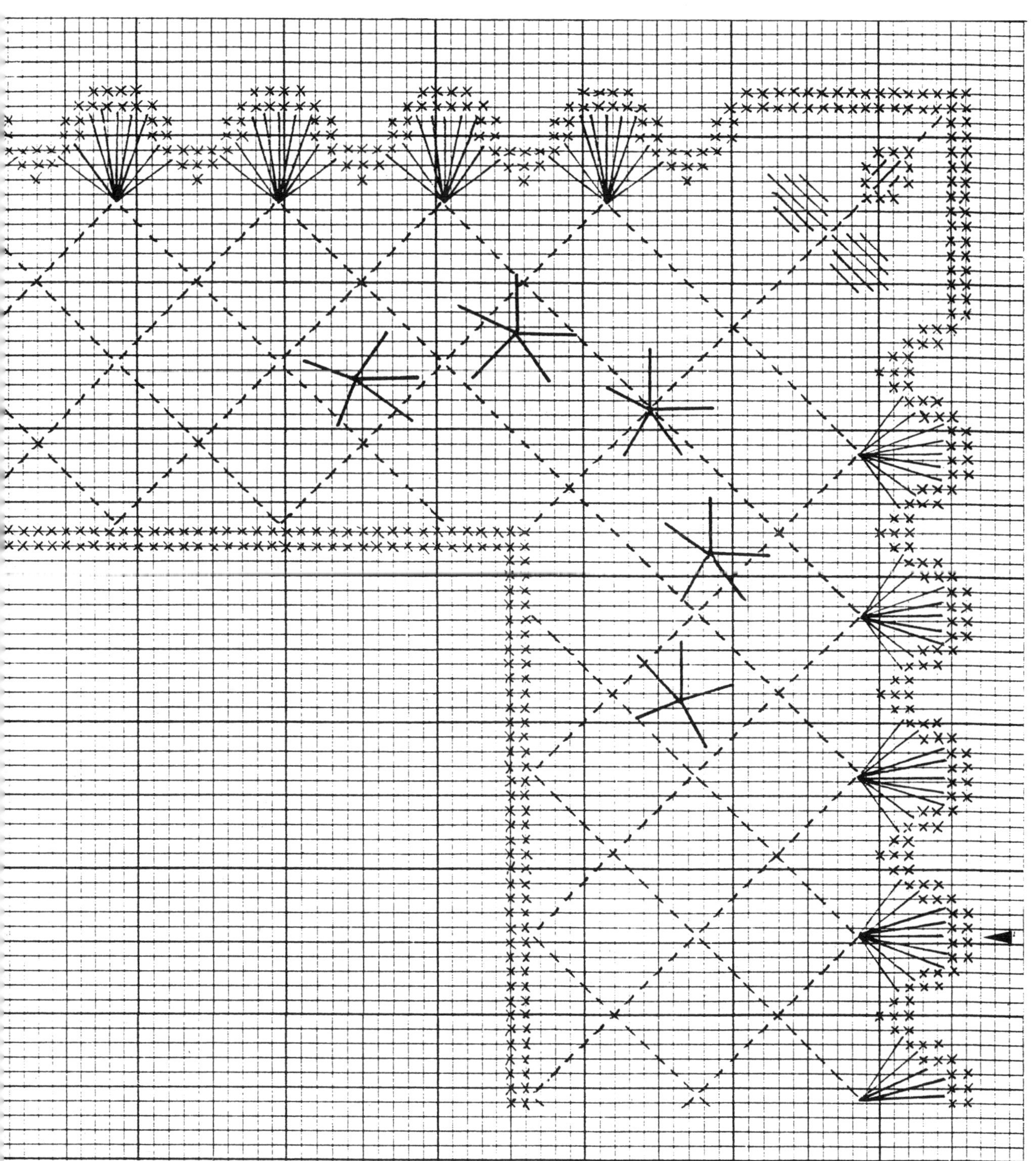

21 *Writing box*

Illustrated on page 54

MATERIALS

Craftwood book box with oval cut-out 10 cm x 14 cm (4" x 5½")
25 cm (10") square pale pink linen-type fabric
Rajmahal Art Silks, 1 skein each:

baby camel 45	barely pink 200
laurel green 65	blue alabaster 201
purple dusk 113	green earth 421
bluebell 121	melaleuca 802
royal blue 126	verdigris 926

Birch silk ribbon, 1 card each:

pale pink 8	bright yellow 15
pale yellow 13	dark pink 24

light card 11 cm x 15 cm (4½" x 6")
thin wadding 11 cm x 15 cm (4½" x 6")

1. For best results, work the embroidery in a hoop. Trace the actual size pattern and transfer it to the centre of the fabric. Following the stitch and colour key diagrams, embroider the motif, starting with the leaves and working the ribbon flowers last. Use 2 strands of silk thread throughout, except for the stems, which are worked using 1 strand of thread only, and the calyx and sepals of each rosebud, which use 3 strands.
2. If worked in a hoop, the embroidery should not need to be pressed before mounting. If it does need pressing, take care not to flatten the ribbon work.
3. Decorate the book box in the finish of your choice. Start by taking off all the hinges and clasps, and removing the panel underneath the lid. Paint the individual pieces and allow to dry thoroughly.*
4. Using the book box lid as a template, draw an oval on the piece of white card and cut 5 mm (3/8") outside the marked line. Glue the wadding to one side of the cardboard oval and allow to dry. Trim to the edge of the card. Centre the card over the wrong side of the embroidery and trim the edges of the fabric 2 cm (¾") outside the oval. Glue these turnings to the back of the card as smoothly as possible. Position the embroidered panel on the back panel of the lid insert so that it will be properly centred in the opening and glue lightly in place. Screw the back panel to the underside of the box lid and re-assemble the box.

* My box was given a coat of sealer, followed by two or three coats of cream folk art paint. A mixture of pink and warm white, incompletely blended, was then sponged all over the front and back covers. The inside of the box was coated in rich gold, and the edges of the oval cut-out were also finished in gold. The sides of the box were dry-brushed with gold to imitate page edges and the spine was given several coats of coffee-bean brown. After being allowed to dry completely, the entire box was varnished.

Key

Oval leaves
satin stitch, melaleuca 802
satin stitch, verdigris 926

Ferns: feather stitch, green earth 421

Lavender: bullion stitch, 5 wraps, purple dusk 113

Bow
centre knot: satin stitch, royal blue 126
front loops: satin stitch, blue alabaster 201
back loops: satin stitch, bluebell 121
ribbon tails: satin stitch, bluebell 121

Stems
1, 3 & 5: stem stitch, laurel green 65
2 & 4: stem stitch, melaleuca 802
all other stems: straight stitch, laurel green 65
small leaves: lazy daisy, melaleuca 802

Rosebuds
petals: lazy daisy, dark pink ribbon 24
calyx: fly stitches: two outside petal loops, one on top; straight stitch in centre over ribbon; melaleuca 802
stem: stem stitch, melaleuca 802

Daisies
petals: straight stitch, pale yellow ribbon 13, bright yellow ribbon 15
centres: French knots, 1 wrap, baby camel 45

Spider's web roses
foundation: 1 strand barely pink 200

centre: dark pink ribbon 24
outer petals: pale pink ribbon 8

Stitch and colour placement guide

Tracing pattern

ACTUAL SIZE

22 Notebook cover *Illustrated on page 54*

MATERIALS

notebook 15 x 21.5 cm (6" x 8½")
50 cm x 30 cm (20" x 12") bright dark mauve silk fabric
35 cm x 30 cm (13½" x 12") lining fabric
35 cm x 30 cm (13½" x 12") thin wadding
32.5 cm x 21.5 cm (12¾" x 8½") thin card
18 cm x 15 cm (7" x 6") iron-on Vilene
7 mm (¼") satin ribbon, 3 m (3½ yds) each:
ivory lavender blue dark rose pink
Rajmahal Art Silks, 1 skein each:
laurel green 65 melaleuca 802 sassafras 805
gilt charm, woman's hand 5 cm (2") long
7 small dark rose pink rosebuds
5 small white ribbon roses
3 small pink ribbon roses
40 cm (16") white guipure lace
40 cm (16") antique gold braid 5 mm (3/16") wide
1 reel gold Rajmahal Hand Sewing Thread

1. Prepare the panel of ribbon weaving. Trace the pattern for the oval onto the Vilene, and place it with the glue side uppermost on an ironing board.
2. Starting with the ivory ribbon, lay it across the oval with one edge against one arm of the cross. Hold the end of the ribbon in place by stabbing a pin through it into the ironing board, about 5 cm (2") outside the edge of the oval. Cut the ribbon 5 cm (2") outside the opposite edge of the shape and leave this end free.
3. Repeat step 2 with the dark rose pink ribbon, aligning the edge of the ribbon with the edge of the ivory ribbon. Continue adding ribbons in each of the three colours in turn, working from the centre to the outer edges until the shape is filled.
4. Start pinning ribbons in the opposite direction in the same way, lining them up with the other arm of the cross on the Vilene.
5. When the second layer is complete, start at one edge and weave each ribbon in turn under and over the ribbons

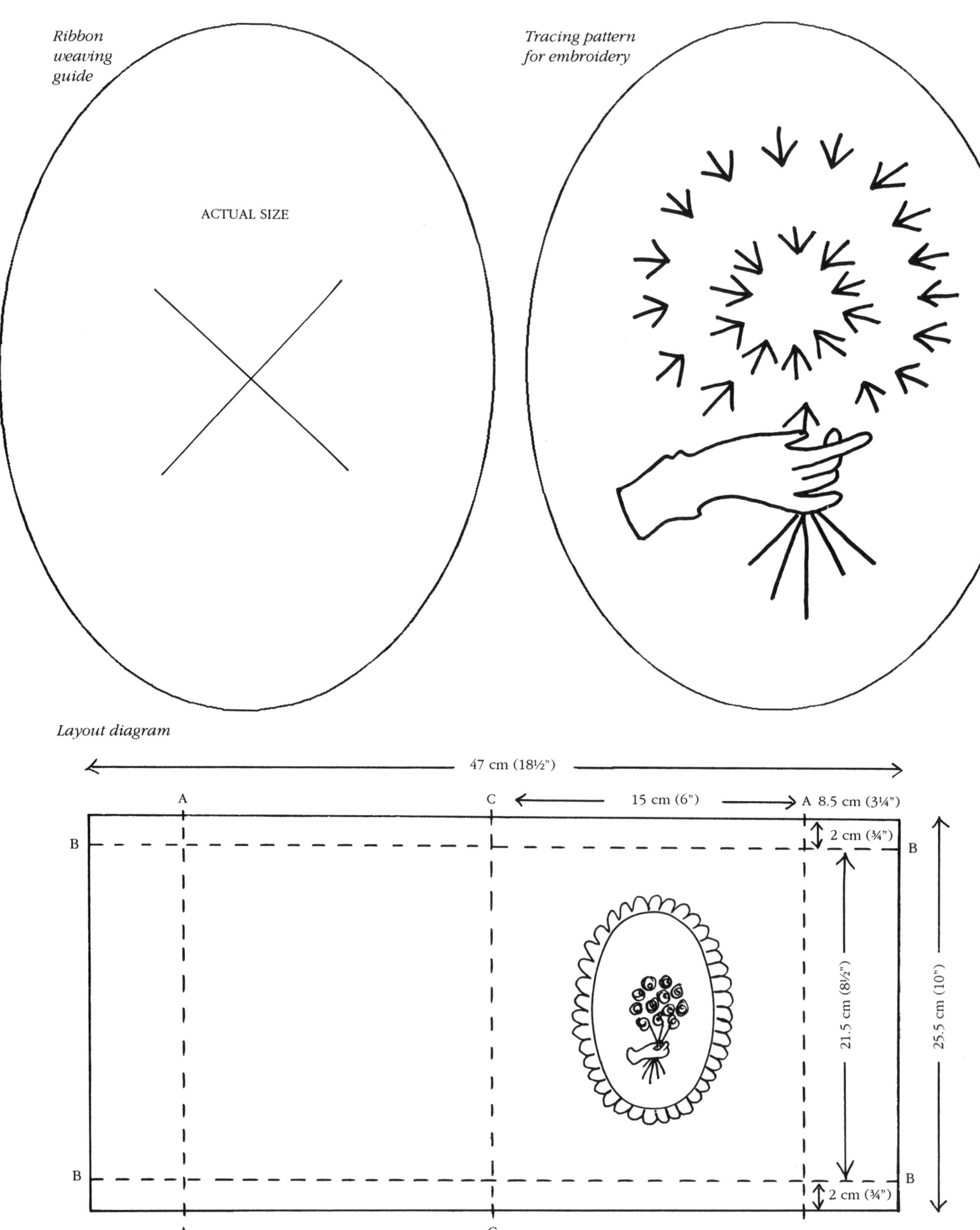
Ribbon weaving guide
ACTUAL SIZE
Tracing pattern for embroidery
Layout diagram
47 cm (18½")
A
C
15 cm (6")
A 8.5 cm (3¼")
B
2 cm (¾")
B
21.5 cm (8½")
25.5 cm (10")
B
B
2 cm (¾")
A
C
A

in the opposite direction, going under the first one on each alternate row. Pin down each end as the weaving is completed.

6. Gently ease the ribbons into place so that they lie flat and straight, then heat the iron and fuse them to the Vilene. Using an appliqué mat during this step will protect the ribbons from excessive heat and prevent the iron picking up any glue.

7. Once the glue has started to take effect, remove the pins carefully and finish off by turning the piece over and pressing it on the wrong side. Allow to cool.

8. Machine a line of straight stitch around the marked oval, with a line of zig-zag stitches just outside it. Trim away the excess fabric outside the stitching and neaten the zig-zagged edge if necessary.

9. Neaten the raw edges of the silk fabric and mark the dotted lines indicated on the layout diagram with tacking stitches or washable pen. Centre the ribbon weaving between the dotted lines on the front, and pin in place, stitching it to the silk by hand or machine through the edge.

10. Slip stitch lace around the outer edge of the oval, covering the edge; if necessary, stitch down the outer edge of the lace (each of the flowers on the cover on page 54 has been anchored with a pearl bead through its centre).

11. Transfer the embroidery pattern to the ribbon-weave oval and work the stem lines in stem stitch, using 3 strands of thread and each of the 3 green silks in turn. Sew 3-strand lazy daisy stitches at each of the lines marked in the top half of the pattern, mixing the greens at random.

12. Glue a scrap of braid to the cuff edge of the hand motif and position it as marked on the pattern. Anchor in place with stitches around the wrist and fingers, using 1 strand of gold thread.

13. Remove the small lengths of green ribbon from the base of each of the roses and rosebuds and arrange the flowers over the stitched area. Sew in place separately, using matching sewing cotton.

14. Complete the embroidery by slip stitching the antique gold braid around the edge of the oval, covering the straight edge of the lace.

15. Finish the raw edges on the short sides of the rectangle of silk fabric with a narrow hem.

16. Following the layout diagram, fold the main fabric piece along the lines marked A with right sides together, and pin in place top and bottom.

17. Mark the centre line C on both the main fabric and the lining, then finish the short sides of the lining with a narrow hem. Position the lining on top of the main fabric, right sides together, matching the centre lines. The lining should just reach the *edges* of the folds at A. Pin the wadding to the wrong side of the silk fabric through all layers.

18. Stitch across the top and bottom on lines marked B, then turn the completed work to the right side.

19. Trim the thin card to exactly the same measurements as the notebook cover, and lightly score lines to bend it around the spine. Push the piece of card into the envelope formed between the wadding and the lining. Turn over the end flaps on the lines marked A to enclose the lining and card completely and form pockets to hold the notebook.

20. Slip notebook into place.

23 *Miniature garden scenes*

Illustrated on page 63

MATERIALS

3 small picture frames, 12 cm x 8 cm (4¾" x 3¼") or frame in 3 parts
20 cm x 40 cm (8" x 16") natural coloured linen
Anchor stranded cotton, 1 skein each:
- pink 036
- cream 275
- brown 906

Gumnut Threads 'Buds' silk, 1 skein each:
- pink 075
- brown 968
- green 584
- white 991

Rajmahal Handsew Metallic Thread:
- silver
- gold

Madeira Silk, 1 packet each:
- emerald 1312
- green 1408

Minnamurra Threads Stranded Cotton, 1 skein each:
- blue/purple MT10
- blue/mauve MT130
- pink/yellow MT50
- yellow/green MT180
- blue/green MT120
- green/brown MT200

Rajmahal Art Silk, 1 skein each:
- barely pink 200
- maidenhair 521
- dusky rose 241
- melaleuca 802
- green earth 421
- sassafras 805

Note: Because of the small amounts required, these little projects are ideal for using up threads left over from other projects.

1. Trace the patterns of the three garden scenes and transfer them to the strip of linen fabric.

2. Work one scene at a time, following the stitch and colour guides. Allow stitches to encroach on adjoining areas to achieve a realistic look. Work the stitches irregularly, changing directions, piling them up on top of one another.

3. Press the embroidery lightly on the wrong side before framing.

Tracing patterns (actual size) with stitch and colour placement guides

1. Conifers

Larger tree, left side: straight stitch, Madeira 1312, 1 strand
Larger tree, right side: straight stitch, Madeira 1408, 1 strand
Blending/shading of tree: straight stitch, Minnamurra MT200, 1 strand
Smaller tree, base: straight stitch, Minnamurra MT120, 1 strand
Smaller tree, shading: straight stitch, Rajmahal 805, 2 strands
Grasses, left hand side: straight stitch, Minnamurra MT180, 2 strands
Foreground: seeding, Rajmahal 421, 2 strands
Flower group 1, leaves: lazy daisy, Rajmahal 521, 2 strands
Flower group 1, flowers: French knots, Minnamurra MT 130, 2 strands
Flower group 2, leaves: buttonhole groups, Rajmahal 805, 2 strands
Flower group 2, flowers: straight stitch stars, Rajmahal 200, 2 strands
Flower group 3, leaves: fly stitch, Minnamurra MT180, 2 strands
Flower group 3, flowers: French knots, Minnamurra MT10, 2 strands
Flower group 4, leaves: bullion stitch, Madeira 1312, 1 strand
Flower group 4, flowers: bullion stitch, Minnamurra MT50, 2 strands
Ferns, right hand side: feather stitch, Rajmahal 802, 2 strands

2. Fountain

Paving slab outlines: back stitch, Anchor 275, 2 strands
Paving slab fillings: seeding, Gumnut 968, 1 strand
Fountain, satin stitch: Gumnut 991, 1 strand
Water: back stitch, Rajmahal silver, 1 strand
Hollyhock stems & leaves: back stitch, Madeira 1408, 1 strand
Centre flower buds: French knots, Gumnut 075, 1 strand
Centre open flowers: buttonhole wheels, Gumnut 075, 1 strand
Outer flower buds: French knots, Minnamurra MT130, 1 strand
Outer open flowers: buttonhole wheels, Minnamurra MT130, 1 strand
Border plant foliage: lazy daisy, Gumnut 584, 1 strand
Border plant flowers: French knots, Minnamurra MT10, 1 strand

3. Blossom tree

Tree trunk & branches: stem stitch, Anchor 906, 2 strands
Blossoms: lightly scatter these four stitches in turn across the shape, building up a rich texture and colour pattern:
first layer: fly stitch, Rajmahal 241, 2 strands
second layer: lazy daisy, Anchor 36, 1 strand
third layer: French knots, Rajmahal 200, 2 strands
fourth layer: seeding, Rajmahal gold, 1 strand
Long grasses: straight stitch, Minnamurra MT180, 2 strands
Foreground grass: seeding, Rajmahal 421, 2 strands

The stitches

Back stitch

Work from right to left. Start by bringing the needle up through the fabric a stitch-length in from the end of the line to be embroidered, and put the needle back down into the fabric right at the end of the line. The second stitch is made by bringing the thread through a stitch-length to the left, and inserting the needle into the hole at the start of the previous stitch.

Basketweave tent stitch

Work in diagonal rows from the top right to the bottom left of the canvas over all intersections. The stitch takes its name from the pattern made on the back of the work; it is the basic 'tapestry' stitch used on canvas.

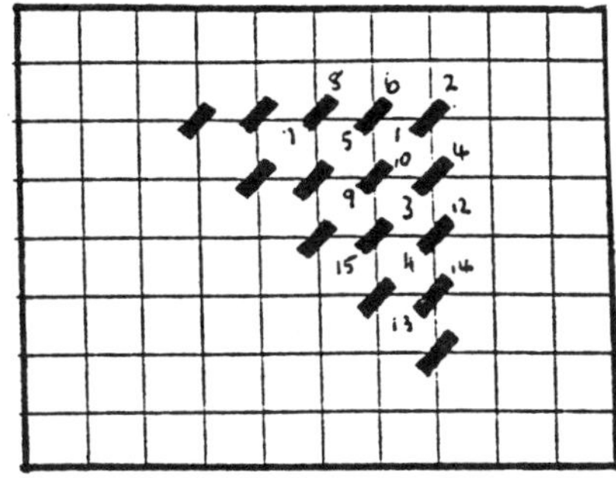

Bullion stitch

A single bullion stitch is worked as shown in the diagram. Bring the thread out at point B then take the needle to point A and insert it through the fabric, coming out again at point B. Wrap the thread firmly but not tightly over the point of the needle several times, until the wraps equal the length of the space between A and B. Holding the wrapped thread down firmly with your thumb, pull the needle through the loops and gently stroke the wrapped thread into place.

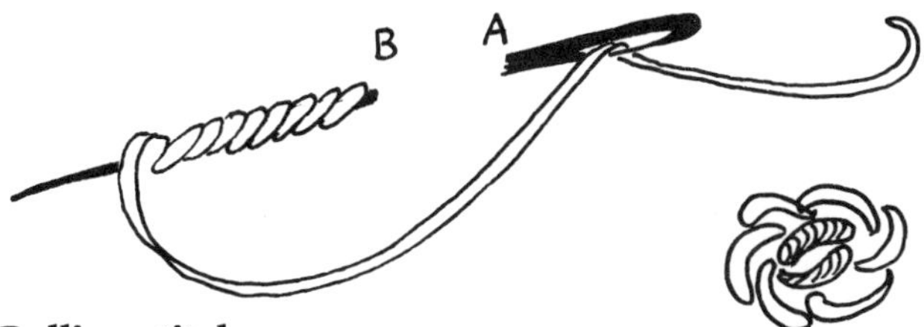

Bullion stitch roses

The rose is constructed of a number of bullion stitches. Start in the centre with 2 stitches in a darker colour lying next to each other, and surround them with a spiral formation of about 5 stitches in a lighter tone.

Buttonhole stitch

Work from left to right. The needle is inserted through the fabric, coming out at the base of the stitch, with the thread loop passing underneath it. Each successive stitch is placed close to the one before; the loops form a tight edge along one side of the row of stitches.

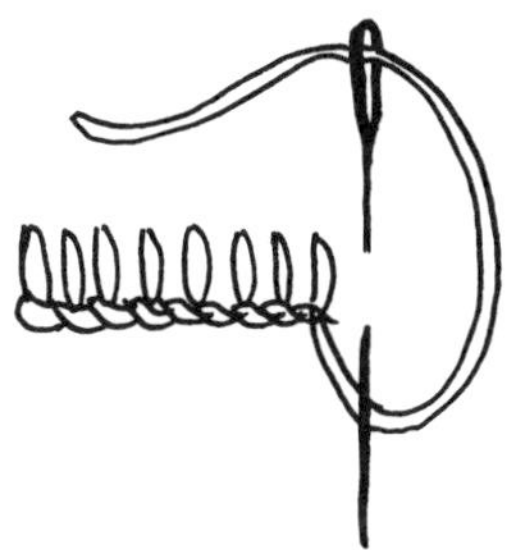

Buttonhole stitch groups

Four or five stitches share a central starting point. The last loop in each group is caught down with a short straight stitch.

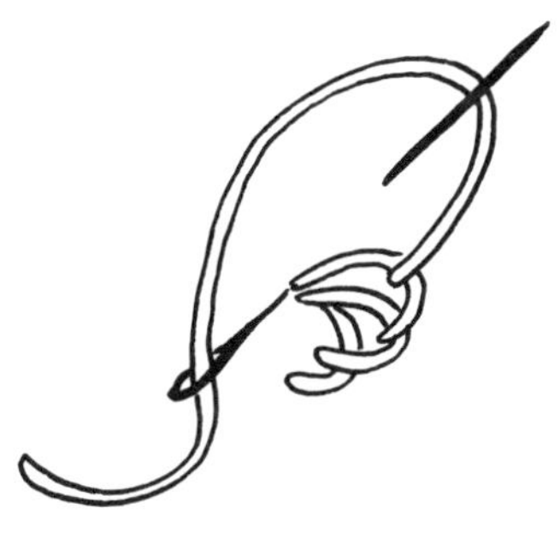

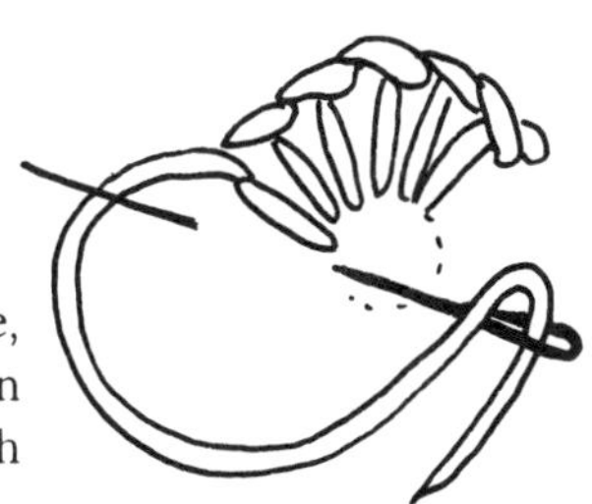

Buttonhole stitch wheels

The stitches are worked in a circle, with the final stitch taken down through the loop of the first stitch made to complete the wheel.

Cable (smocking)

Work from left to right. With the needle held at right angles to the pleats and parallel to the pleating thread, bring the thread up from behind the fabric, and take the needle through the next pleat to the right from right to left. Keeping the thread *above* the needle, pull it through to tighten

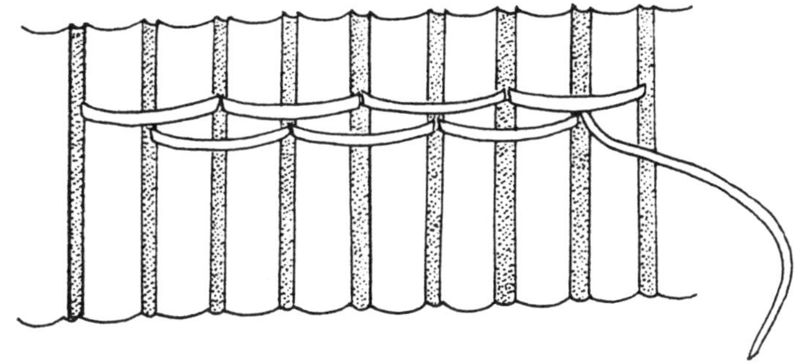

the stitch across the two pleats. The second stitch is made by taking the needle through the next pleat from right to left, but with the thread passing *below* the needle. Continue in this way across the row of pleats, alternating the position of the thread on each stitch. Use the pleating thread as a guide to keep the line of stitches straight.

Cable floret (smocking)
A group of six cable stitches is worked over the central pleats in a motif to give a floral effect. Further stitches can be added below the flowers in green cotton to represent leaves.

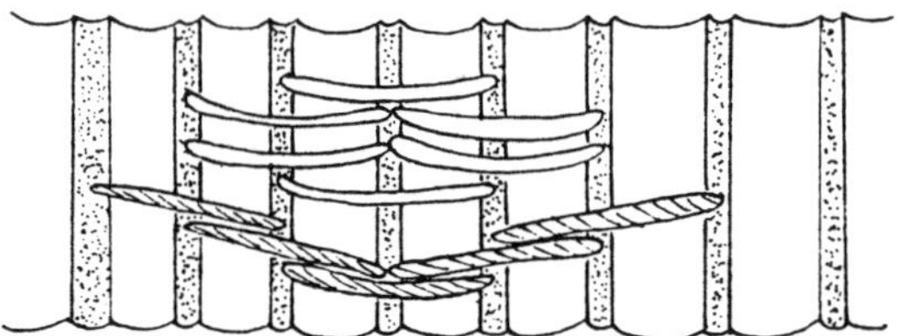

Chain stitch
Start by bringing the needle out at the beginning of the line to be worked. The needle is put back into the same hole, and the point is taken out again a short distance below, with the yarn passing underneath it. Pulling the needle through forms a loop. The next stitch is made in the same way, with the needle entering the fabric inside the loop at the point where the yarn emerges.

Chain stitch filling
Chain stitch is worked in lines close together to fill a shape.

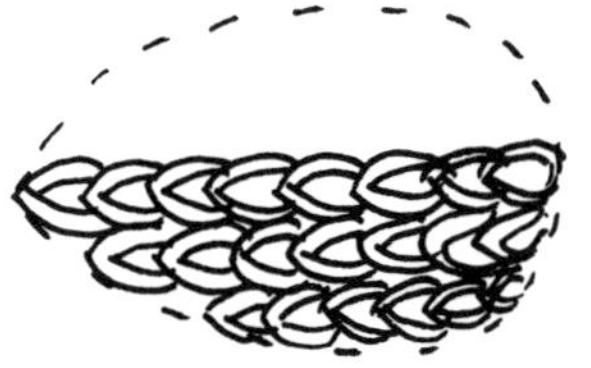

Couching
Small stitches are taken at intervals along a length of thread or cord laid across the background fabric to hold it in place.

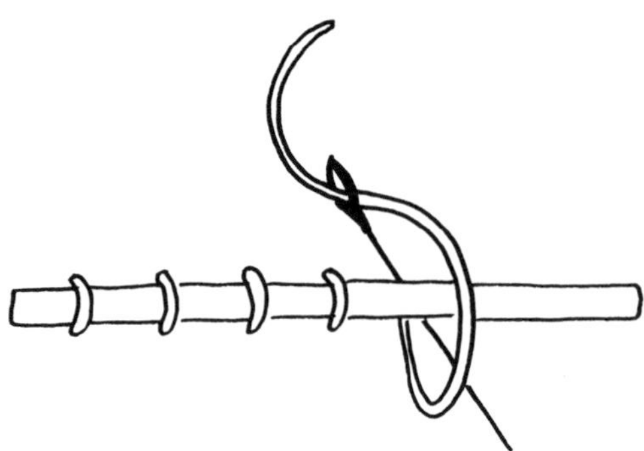

Cross-stitch
This stitch can be worked in rows by embroidering the first stitches in a line from left to right, then working back in the opposite direction to complete the row, or as single stitches. For large areas it is better to work in rows, as the finished effect tends to be smoother. When working with variegated threads, however, it is advisable to make each stitch individually to preserve the subtle colour changes in the thread.

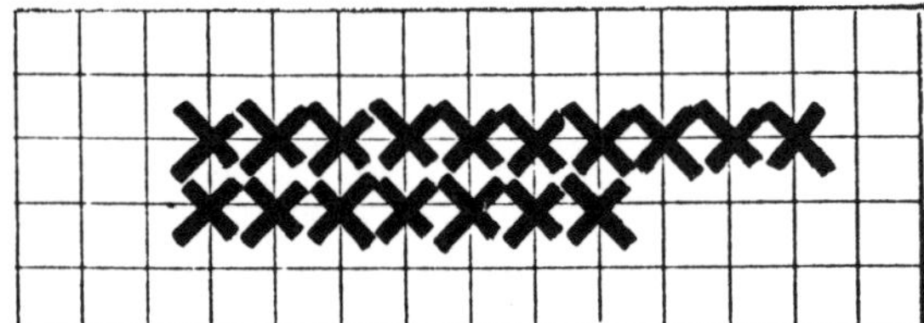

Eyelet stars
These consist of a group of straight stitches radiating from a central point. If the thread is pulled tight, a hole will appear in the centre of the stitches.

Feather stitch
This is worked similarly to buttonhole stitch, but the stitches are made alternately on either side of a central line.

Fishbone stitch
Used mainly to fill leaf shapes. Start with a small straight stitch along the centre line. Bring the needle out on the right hand edge of the shape close to the top of the straight stitch, and insert it again at the bottom of the stitch on the other side of the centreline. The next stitch is made in the same way, but from the left side of the leaf, crossing the first at the centreline. The stitches can also be taken right across the shape, which creates a much more solid raised effect.

Fly stitch
Each stitch is basically an open loop caught in place with a small straight stitch. The size and direction of the stitches can be varied in creative embroidery; piling the individual stitches on top of one another, working each layer in different shades of thread, is an excellent way to represent foliage. Used as the calyx for a rosebud, the anchoring stitch can be elongated to form a stem. The stitch can also be worked in groups to represent leaves; in this case, the anchoring stitches become the central vein.

French knots

The needle is brought out at the desired point, and the thread is wrapped around the point one or more times anticlockwise. The point of the needle is put into the fabric close to the starting point, and the loops are held down firmly with the thumbnail of the non-working hand while the needle is pulled through to the wrong side.

Interlocking star stitch

Make a long stitch and work another of equal length to cross it in the middle at right angles. Work two diagonal stitches over the first to produce an eight-pointed star. Bring the needle up slightly to the side of the centre point and take a very small stitch over all the intersecting threads. Fasten off.

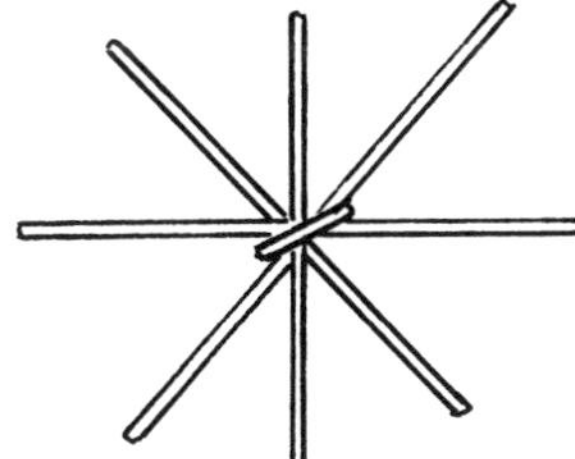

Ladder stitch

Ladder stitch is worked in a sewing thread which matches the material as closely as possible. The needle is slid through the fold on one edge for about 2 mm, then a horizontal stitch is taken into the fold of the opposite edge, and the needle passed through that for another 2 mm. The small stitches which connect the two pieces of fabric are almost invisible.

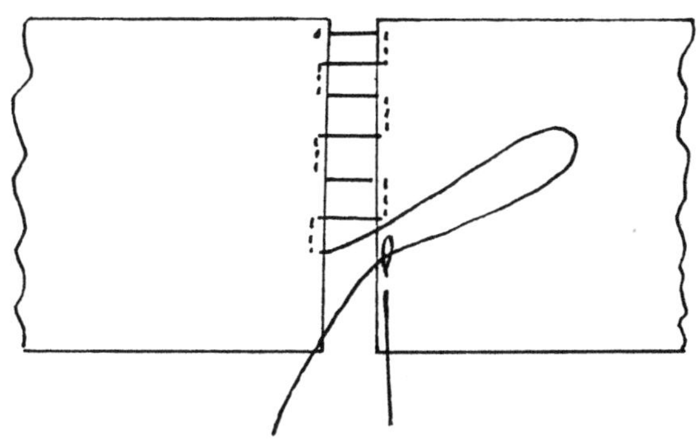

Lazy daisy stitch

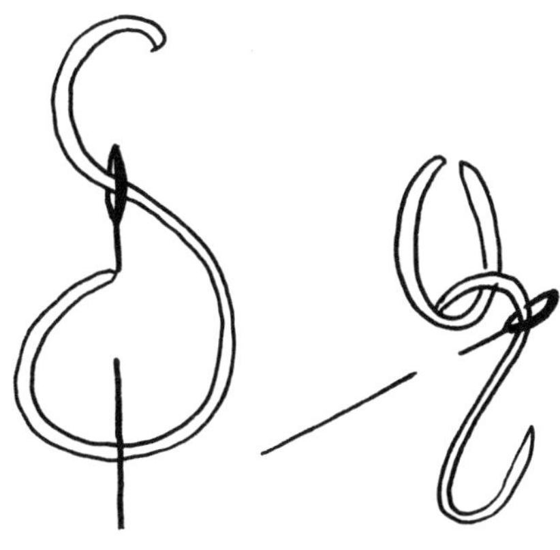

The thread is brought out at the starting point, and the needle inserted in the same hole, emerging a short distance away with the thread looped underneath it. The loop is pulled to lie flat on the fabric, and anchored with a small straight stitch. The stitches can be worked singly or in groups to represent the petals of larger flowers.

Long and short stitch

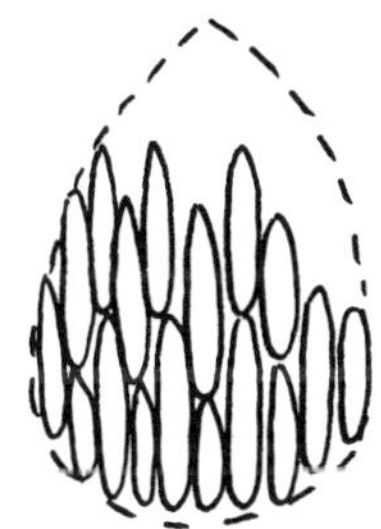

The first row of stitches is worked along the widest point of the shape to be filled, and consists of alternate long and short satin stitches. The remaining rows have stitches all the same length, which follow the bottom line of the previous rows. Shading is achieved by changing the colour used for each row. The angle of the stitches can be changed to fill tapering shapes, and a few straight stitches will fill any gaps which remain.

Padded satin stitch

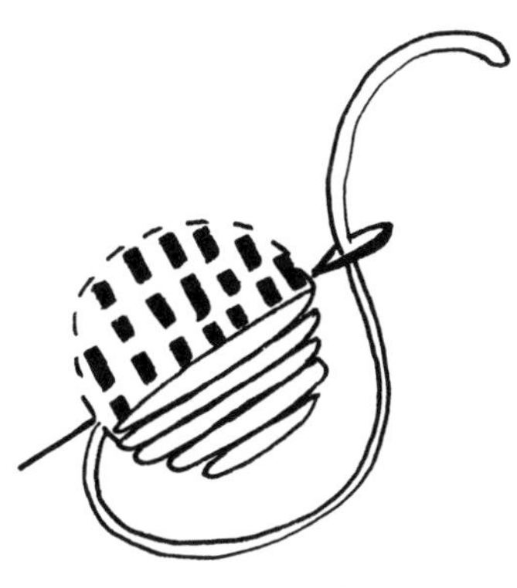

Begin by working rows of running stitch across the shape to be filled, working at right angles to the direction of the overlying satin stitch. The satin stitch is worked over the stitched area in the normal way. When completed, it has a slightly raised appearance.

Raised stem band

This stitch is worked over a foundation which consists either of a number of straight stitches placed close together, or a cord or braid, as in the stem of the Topiary Rose design. The cord is couched down with horizontal straight stitches at regular intervals which form a 'ladder' on which the stem stitch is worked in the normal way, starting at the bottom of the cord. The stitches pass around the horizontal bars, but do not go into the fabric except at the ends. Each subsequent row is worked in the same direction, packed close to the row before, until the entire foundation has been covered completely.

Satin stitch
This is a very useful filling stitch in which long straight stitches are worked next to each other to fill the area being worked. Care should be taken to make sure that the stitches are evenly spaced, just touching each other.

Seeding
Very small straight stitches are placed at random over an area to be filled. Their direction and length can be varied.

Spider's web rose
Five straight stitches are worked in a star shape to form the foundation of these roses. The 'petals' consist of a length of ribbon or thread which is brought up close to the centrepoint, using a blunt needle, and woven under and over alternate spokes of the star until they are completely filled. The thread is taken to the back of the fabric close to the edge of the rose and finished off.

Split stitch
Worked like stem stitch, split stitch differs only in that the needle comes up in the middle of the previous stitch, splitting the fibres. It is best worked in wool, which is soft enough to part easily.

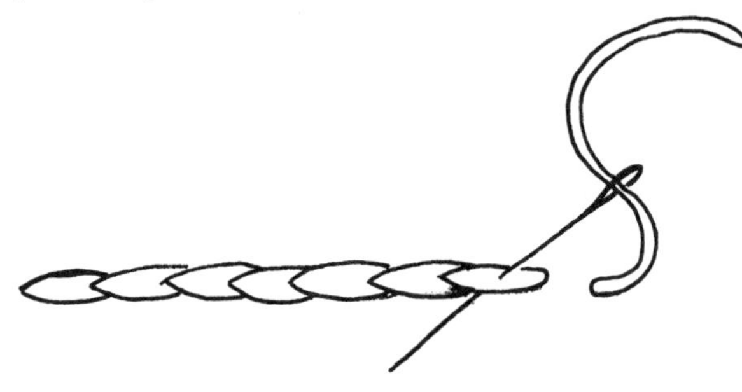

Stem stitch
Start with a small straight stitch, then insert the needle into the fabric half a stitch length from the end of the first stitch, and bring it out next to the first stitch with the loop of thread kept underneath the needle. A line of stitches is produced this way, each overlapping the the previous one.

Straight stitch
Random stitches: can be any length, can point in any direction, and can be worked singly or in groups. Very small straight stitches worked as a filling stitch are called seeding.

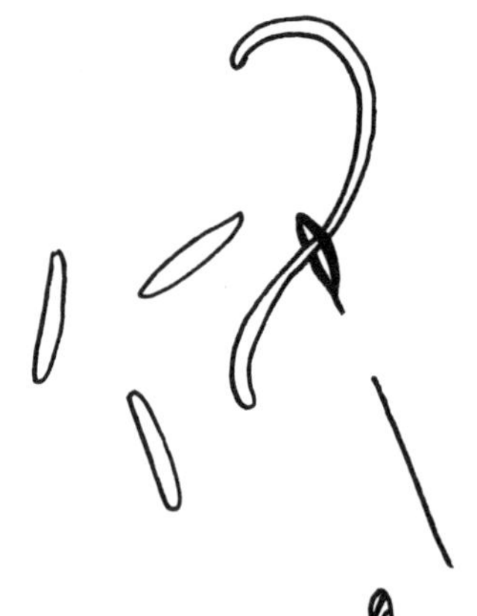

Straight stitch star
Five or six small straight stitches are worked in a circle, sharing the same centre point.

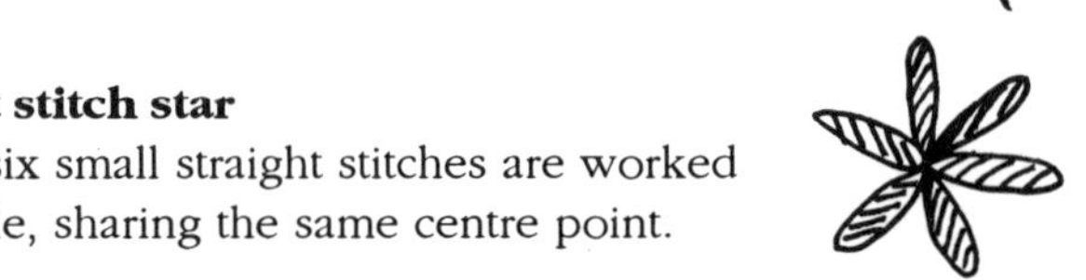

Tent stitch
The basic 'tapestry' stitch; lines of tent stitch can be worked in any direction. Each stitch crosses one intersection of the canvas from top right to bottom left on horizontal rows and bottom left to top right when worked vertically. This produces a long diagonal stitch on the back of the work. Backgrounds and other large areas of stitchery are best worked in the basketweave variation of this stitch illustrated on page 73.

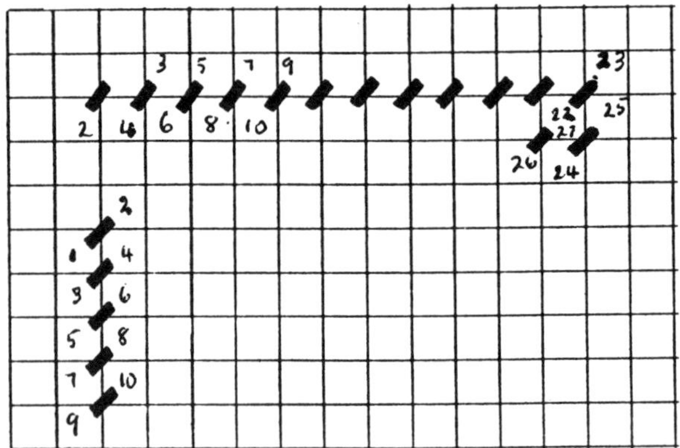

Trellis (smocking)
A method of patterning based on the cable stitch. The lines of stitches are worked up and down between the pleating threads to produce grid patterns.

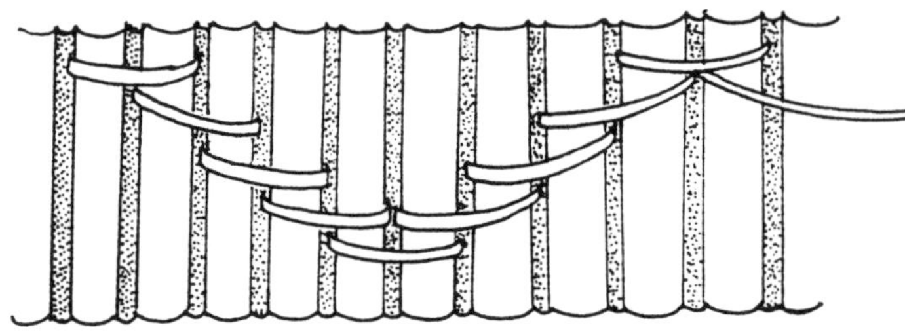

Trellis stitch

Long evenly spaced threads are taken across the shape to be covered, first in one direction, and then the opposite way. A contrasting thread is then used to work a small cross-stitch over each intersection of the threads, holding them down to the foundation fabric. This is best worked in an embroidery frame.

Handy hints

TRANSFERRING PATTERNS TO FABRIC

Several methods can be used to transfer the designs to fabric. The easiest is to place the material on top of the pattern and trace the design with a lead pencil, fade-out pen or wash-out pen.

Transfer pencils, which can be used with tracing paper to make an iron-on transfer, are also available. The pattern should be traced first in pencil, then turned over. Trace it on the reverse side with the transfer pencil, then iron onto the fabric following the manufacturer's directions.

Dressmaker's carbon paper can be used in between the tracing and the fabric, a technique particularly useful on dark fabrics where pen and pencil lines are difficult to see clearly.

Wool fabrics in particular present problems when transferring patterns because of the irregularity of the surface. Make a tracing of the design, then pierce it with a thick needle at regular intervals along all the lines. Pin the pattern to the fabric and mark a dot at each hole with a blue wash-out pen. Remove the pattern and connect the dots to form the pattern lines. Alternatively, pin the pattern to the fabric and transfer the design by stitching tacking stitches in a contrasting colour along all lines. Tear away the tracing paper to leave the stitching as a guide. The tacking stitches are pulled out as each section is worked.

MAKING A TWISTED CORD

Cut the yarn for the cord into lengths three times the finished length required and tie them together at one end with a firm but not tight overhand knot. Anchor the knot with a large pin to a firm surface such as the arm of an upholstered chair, or a large cushion. Take the ends of the yarn and twist them in a clockwise direction, keeping them under slight tension, until the centre of the twisted thread begins to kink slightly.

Fold the end you are holding up to the knot and ease the knot open enough to enable you to slip the end through the loop. Pull the knot tight, then gently work down the length of the cord, making sure that the twists lie across one another smoothly.

To make a tasselled end, tie an overhand knot about 2.5 cm (1") from one end of the cord. Cut the loops and trim the ends even, then fluff out the threads beyond the knot.

FRAMING AN EMBROIDERED PANEL

Measure the finished embroidery and cut a piece of thick cardboard to the exact size. Use a craft knife and a metal-edged ruler to do this as accurately as possible, making sure that the corners are square.

Cut the excess fabric from the edge of the panel, leaving a margin of 5 cm (2") all around for turnings.

Place the embroidery face down on a table and centre the cardboard panel over it. Bring the corners of the fabric over the card and hold them in place with a small blob of glue. Fold the sides of the fabric over, mitring the corners, and pin along the top edge, into the cardboard, to hold the fabric in place. Repeat the pinning with the bottom edge, pulling the fabric tightly across the card in the process, then pin the sides one at a time in the same manner.

The embroidery can now be placed in the frame.

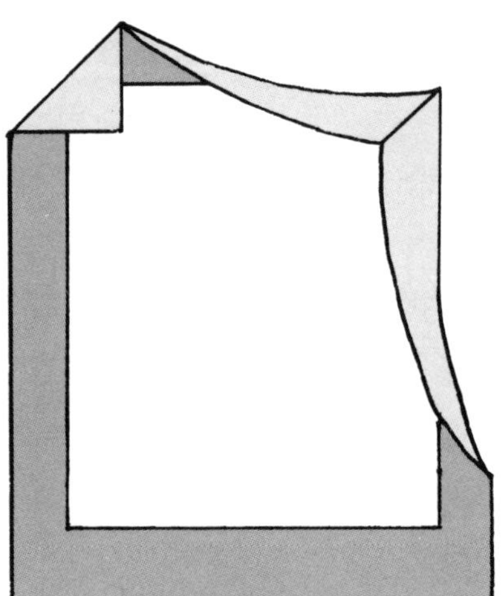

Turn the corners over the edge of the card then turn the fabric over the card

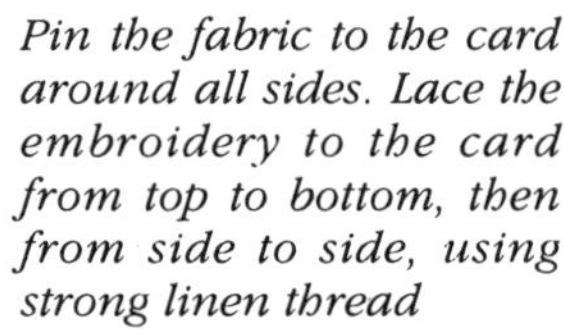

Pin the fabric to the card around all sides. Lace the embroidery to the card from top to bottom, then from side to side, using strong linen thread

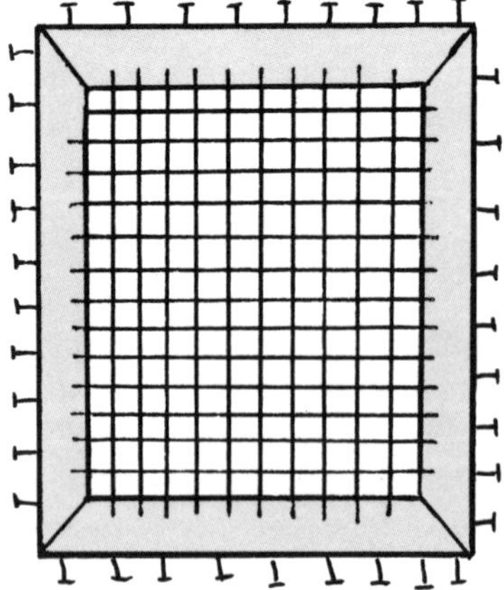

FRENCH SEAMS

Place the two fabric sections to joined, wrong sides together, and sew a seam 7 mm (1/4") from the raw edges. Fold the fabric strip, right sides together, enclosing the raw edges of the seam, and press. Sew a second line of stitches 10 mm (3/8") away from the folded edge. Open fabric out and press seam flat to one side.

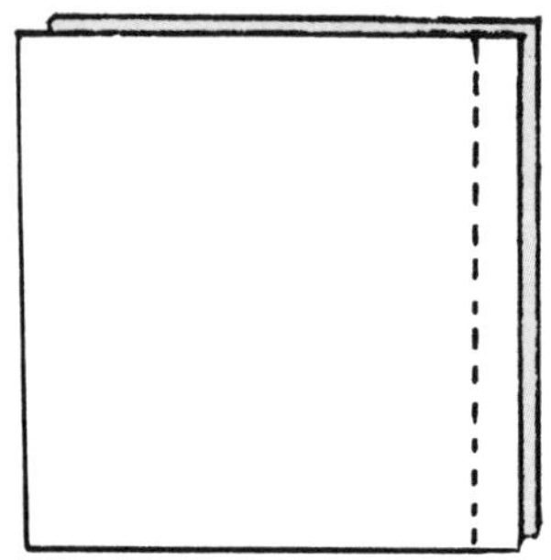

With wrong sides facing, seam the two pieces of fabric together 7 mm (1/4") from the edge

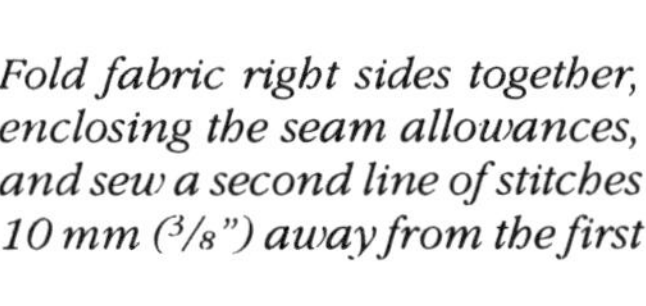

Fold fabric right sides together, enclosing the seam allowances, and sew a second line of stitches 10 mm (3/8") away from the first

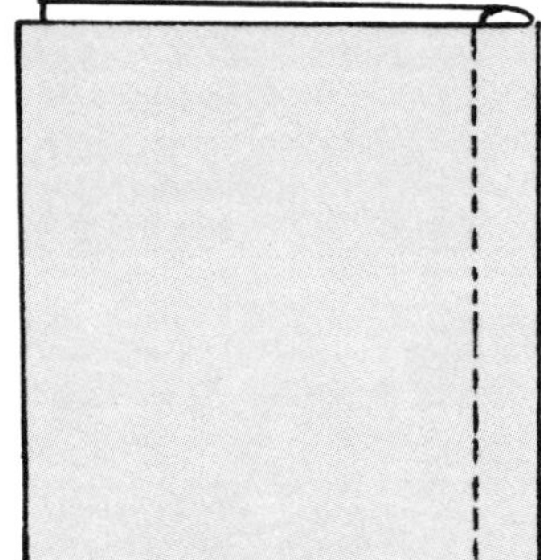

Suppliers

Helen Norton
Creative Craft Kits
PO Box 111
Gordon NSW 2072
Shadow box and chatelaine kits

DMC Needlecraft Pty Ltd
PO Box 317
Earlwood NSW 2206
Threads, fabrics and embroidery equipment

Clifton Joseph and Son
301/393 Little Lonsdale Street
Melbourne Vic 3000
Appletons Crewel Wools

Ireland Needlecraft Pty Ltd
PO 1175
Narrewarren Vic 3805
Framecraft and Sudberry House products, Kreinik metallic threads

Coats Patons Crafts
Private Bag 15
Mulgrave North Vic 3170
Threads

Timberturn Pty Ltd
1 Shepley Avenue
Panorama SA 5041
Wooden box with lid insert

Rajmahal
Fosterville Road
Bagshot East Vic 3551
Art silk, metallic threads, including Sadi and Shisha mirrors

Minnamurra Threads
PO Box 325
Kiama NSW 2533
Variegated stranded and pearl cottons

Gumnut Yarns
PO Box 519
Mudgee NSW 2850
Australian made crewel yarns, silk threads, tapestry wool and mohair blends

Precious Pieces
160B Scarborough Beach Road
Scarborough WA 6019
Craft supplies, materials and classes

DD Creative Crafts
PO Box 565
Ringwood Vic 3134
Perforated paper, Bucilla silk ribbon

Index

Alphabets
  back stitch, 14
  counted thread, 19

Back stitch, 73
Basketweave tent stitch, 73
Blossom tree, 72
Brooch cushion, 34
Bullion stitch, 73
Bullion stitch roses, 73
Buttonhole stitch, 73
  groups, 73
  wheels, 73

Cable (smocking), 73
Cable floret (smocking), 74
Calico mouse, 7
Chain stitch, 74
  filling, 74
Chatelaine, 32
Conifers, 5, 72
Couching, 74
Crazy patchwork box, 22
Crewel work candlescreen, 38
Cross-stitch, 74
  sampler, 19

Embroidered towel edging, 44
Eyelet stars, 74

Feather stitch, 74
Fishbone stitch, 74
Flower trellis cushion, 60
Fly stitch, 74
Fountain, 72
French knots, 75

Heart of roses cushion, 56

Interlocking star stitch, 75
Introduction, 4

Ladder stitch, 75
Lazy daisy stitch, 75
Long and short stitch, 75

Miniature garden scenes, 71

Notebook cover, 69

Oven cloth, 45

Padded satin stitch, 75
Pansy tray cloth, 55
Photo frame mat, 65

Raised stem band, 75
Ribbon weaving, 69
Rose and initial jar lid, 13

Sampler, 19
Satin stitch, 75
Seeding, 76
Shoe sweeteners, 26
Smocked cushion, 62
Spider's web roses, 76
Split stitch, 76
Stem stitch, 76
Stitches, 73
Straight stitch, 76
Straight stitch star, 76
Sweet pea pillowcase, 10

Tapestry box-lid, 35
Tea cosy, 46
Tent stitch, 76
Topiary rose tree, 15
Tray cloth, 55
Trellis
  cushion, 60
  smocking, 76
  stitch, 77

Wisteria shadow box, 5
Writing box, 68